FIRST, The Street Guide to Digital Business Influence
by Dean DeLisle

Digital | 978-1-944027-19-3
Soft | 978-1-944027-18-6

www.networlding.com

I dedicate this to my father, Bob, who has been there since the beginning, and to my loving wife, Holly, who always hangs in there through thick and thin.

TABLE OF CONTENTS

PREFACE

Not too long ago, I created a social networking platform called Social Jack™. It's a 24/7 online resource to help our client thought leaders harness the power of social media. Our entire company is built on the premise that working with social media and building an online influence presence requires constant learning, every day. Then we added an additional element that is essential to building digital business influence: the focus on helping our clients *engage* and *network* successfully with one another and with their respective networks.

One of my main goals with this book is to take you through my own journey to offer you dozens and dozens of honest, deep insights I gathered from years of trial and error. I'm far from an overnight success, but, because of my commitment to constant learning and partnering with other people like myself who held what I call *can-do* attitudes, I'm grateful to say that I have achieved a level of success for which I am most grateful.

Yet, even more importantly, as a result of my success, I'm now able to share with you a large number of secrets, tips, strategies, and tactics, you can use to become *FIRST*. In today's world, the Number One way to accomplish this goal is to master social media. For many of you, that may seem like a daunting task.

The good news though is that I will teach you how to attain a mastery level in no more than twenty minutes a day by using what I call "Power Moves." These moves are one, three, or five-minute exercises.

These moves work, and will prevent you from feeling overwhelmed. So many people – from entrepreneurs to professionals to executives feel bogged down and even stagnant because they don't have good organized, time-tested instruction. They find themselves overdoing, overthinking, and ultimately getting stuck in *analysis paralysis*. I'll show you how to move forward effectively and efficiently. I am honored to be your coach.

The Ascent: How I Became a Digital Business Influencer

Let me start with my work history to give you some context as to who I am and, more importantly, *why* I know I can help you. You see, my own early career path in the restaurant industry led me to the world of social media. Does that seem strange? It's not, really. At the heart of all wildly popular restaurants are certain distinct elements—from the ambiance, to the food, the spices, and, of course, the wait staff. The unique combination of all of these elements creates a perfect blend. This is the "recipe" to success in the restaurant business.

It's also the "recipe" to success in life, sales, and any business. These elements are always in flux, changing from week to week, even from hour to hour. What has that got to do with business influence? Everything. Let me explain.

I began working as a busboy in the restaurant business when I was about thirteen. By observing, constantly listening, and asking lots of questions, I was able to learn a great deal about my boss and coworkers. I also learned a lot about the hospitality business in a short amount of time. This predated the internet and social media by a few decades. But as that young kid, I was fortunate to learn the ropes and the value of networking by observing meetings in the restaurant between business people as well as politicians.

I soon realized that networking is the best path to upward mobility, and career and business success. When social media cropped up and developed into the dominant way of growing one's business and career, it felt like a natural evolution to transfer what I had learned to that space, and to master it.

Along my path, I realized merely connecting with people is not enough. The best end result for all concerned—a win/win—takes place when you *invest time* and *focus* on creating, nurturing, and developing mutually beneficial relationships. This is how I was able to be consistently present with those in my network. I also learned how important it is to be present in your hurt and pain, joy and/or sadness. Be present with your emotions and with the people in your life. That is what both personal and professional relationships are about – presence.

From my humble start as a busboy to eventually becoming the CEO of my own global social media training organization, I learned that forming long-lasting relationships also creates a fertile base upon which to build a solid networking team for myself and those in my network. I saw that rather than using others as stepping-stones to get to my next benchmark and then leaving them behind, I could take my network with me, and we could all prosper.

Also, with my restaurant roots, I found myself spending a lot of time in the kitchen, learning from the chefs how to create wonderful dishes at home. I began to use the metaphor of recipe creation to explain how I was growing all of my ventures.

Those early years as a busboy taught me the art of building relationships that would turn into additional recipes for success. Today, my metaphoric recipes have helped me achieve success in the fields of business systems, flipping houses, and starting and building my own companies. With every venture I've undertaken, I've focused on creating the best recipes for success, but I also know that with each recipe there is always room for improvement.

When a new flavor or spice becomes available (for example, in the form of new ideas or new people) I add those new elements to my *recipes* to improve them. I continue to be adamant about developing the best recipes for success, for myself and for others. So this book is really a recipe book on how you can take the best strategies, tactics, and my streetwise insights to master digital business influence.

From all my life's learnings, I've aggregated recipes for success with the hope that you'll have all the upsides with little or no downsides. I'll share with you my time-tested recipes to build your network to become *FIRST*, the gift that keeps on giving to you and all those you know.

INTRODUCTION:
MY *FIRST* REALIZATION
of Business Influence

Tell Your Story

One of the most important recipes for digital business success is your own story. I'm talking about your authentic story—the true story about you, not one some marketing manager creates. Our authentic stories aren't just about showing other people who we truly are. They're also about revealing our passions so people can better connect with us. People connect with us when they understand why we do what we do, and where our passions lie. To provide you with this framework, here's my story.

I was born in 1962. My first home was an Indiana farmhouse. From the time I could first walk, I remember wanting to escape. In fact, my parents would regularly find their toddler half a mile down the road from our home, going who knows where.

As the years passed, I constantly felt I wanted to run away, to be anyplace but where I was at that time. This was a recurring theme in my formative years. I felt like I didn't belong. I was always looking for someplace where I could achieve acceptance and experience a richer sense of community.

My dad was an Air Force Special Forces pilot. My mother was from England. Our family was the two of them, me, and my baby sister, Desiree. When I was three years old, for whatever reason, my parents decided to move to Australia. We shipped all our belongings across the world except for a few clothes and other small things we could pack and carry. For me, this move meant losing sight and possession of my favorite toys. On the way to relocating Down Under, we first stopped in England at my mom's parents' house to visit with them. Shortly thereafter, my dad developed severe, debilitating stomach ulcers. As a result, we never got to Australia.

This was a big deal to me because now I had permanently lost everything that I had ever collected up to that point in my life, except for what remained in my luggage. I really missed my toys and hated having to start over. I know my gloomy attitude put even more stress and strain on my parents, given everything the two of them had lost.

Starting over in a foreign country, I became "the kid with the funny accent." I worked hard to connect and develop friends, but it wasn't easy. By the time I entered first grade, I would often be running wild around the streets of London. Very "Oliver Twist"—a renegade little kid scrambling around with almost no supervision. I remember running with a small pack of kids who were my friends and allies, no matter what. Thankfully, I had the gift of gab even then.

I enjoyed talking to street merchants and other locals. I knew all the cops, who, in England, are typically called "bobbies." They were often kind enough to make sure I got home safely. They probably wondered why my parents didn't keep closer tabs on me. However, they never acted like I was a nuisance, and I will always be grateful to them for that. I got to know many of them personally over time. They felt like a solid network of protection when needed. My hunger to connect with others for a variety of reasons kept growing at an insatiable rate.

After about three years in England, my parents split up. Dad brought Desiree and me back to the United States. Mom was very young, and being back in her homeland around her parents and friends apparently made her realize that she simply wasn't up for marriage and kids at that time. With whatever money Dad had in his pocket, back to the Midwest we went. Once again, everything I had collected for the last three years of my life was abandoned.

Upon our return we moved in with my father's parents in Calumet City on the south side of Chicago. That house was brimming with people, including Desiree, my dad, his youngest brothers, my grandparents, and me—all under one roof. It was a snug environment, but one filled with love, fun, and the warmth of family. I felt protected, loved, and wanted. Even though we had to sleep three to a bed nightly, I felt a rich sense of family and teamwork.

Soon I was enrolled in school, and once again, I was the kid with the funny accent - this time because I had picked up some influence from the Brits' lingo while living over there. I got picked on, but now I was bigger and no longer afraid to fight back. I was an angry little guy at that point. My dad's brothers were closer to my age, so they were more like older brothers than uncles. They looked out for me and bailed me out of dicey situations quite a few times.

Eventually, I started making friends and began learning how to fit in. Around that time, my dad married a wonderful Dutch-German woman. She quickly became "mom" to my sister and me, as the memory of our birth mother gradually faded. When I turned seven, we moved to Hammond, a suburb of Gary, Indiana. Ours was a good house, but was situated in a rough area in one of the poorer sections of town.

At the end of our block was a country club. It was an anomaly, given the adjoining neighborhood. On my morning paper route, I rode my bike down to the fence surrounding the club entrance, telling myself that *someday, I'll be a member there.* That was an early vision of mine. I had seen the many nice cars and well-dressed people who were members of that club and could picture myself as one of them. Not that I didn't have clothes, but mine usually had patches. I was a rough-and-tumble kid, definitely a handful.

Entrepreneurial Beginnings

My dad was quite entrepreneurial, always selling something on the side while working whatever regular job he had. He was also going to night school to get his degree, so he didn't have a lot of time to spend with me. My new mom had her master's degree and was an elementary school teacher. She was adamant about having a good work ethic. I remember her working night and day, while directing us to complete a variety of household chores in between our play. "Work hard for what you want" was the directive that my family drilled into me early on.

One of my own first entrepreneurial ventures was running a local neighborhood kids' carnival once or twice a year. A buddy and I would make signs and post them all over the place. Our parents took turns letting us use their garages.

We showed eight-millimeter home movies, put on animal shows, and had games where the kids could win little prizes (usually unwanted items that would have otherwise been sold in a garage sale or donated to Goodwill). We sold tickets, popcorn, and lemonade. I don't know how much we made, but it was always fun and provided a supplement to my allowance. Suffice it to say that at a young age, I had figured out how to make money.

Time marched on and I kept looking for new ways to make money. For example, my mom got me into stamp collecting, which was very big at that time. The pictures on the stamps always fascinated me because I wanted to travel the world. You could buy international stamps fairly cheaply where I could see pictures of amazing faraway places. The Walter Mitty side of me fed my imagination, and though it certainly wasn't feasible then, I felt I would travel the world someday. It was a fantastic daydream.

Life was always a grand adventure. I looked forward to the next unique thing or special event I could attend. I constantly had a deep yearning to keep exploring opportunities that might lead me closer to my dreams. I also wanted to escape the pain of my birth mother not wanting me. (Today, this might be classified as attachment theory). I was not only looking for somewhere else, but also for others to love and accept me. I don't believe I even knew how recognize when love and outreach was right in front of me. I have no doubt my dad and family loved me, but for whatever reasons, I couldn't experience it, not the way I imagined it would feel.

But back to my budding entrepreneurial drive. My stepmom inspired me to create a stamp company. Here, around age eleven, I developed an inventory-control system. I was purchasing and packaging stamps, and then reselling them. She even had me give talks to the kids at her school about stamps. I sold them stamp kits so they could start collecting. Who knew at the time that presentation and sales would become my future? I can honestly say my career in seminar selling started right then and there.

Hospitality Training

As I got older, naturally I wanted to make more money. Whenever my parents could afford it, they would take us to one of the nicest restaurants in town, Freddy's Steakhouse. When we showed up, we would always sit in the same booth and the same waitress would take care of us. We were regulars, and they treated us well.

I still habitually frequent restaurants where I'm a regular. I ask for the same servers, have a specific table, and enjoy seeing my servers' faces brighten when they see me. They step forward quickly to greet me warmly. This was another example of life's little but meaningful perks I created, as it served to fulfill my desire to *belong*.

Then when I was about thirteen, we were sitting in our booth one summer evening. It was next to the restaurant owner's office. The idea suddenly hit me that this would be a great place to work. I liked the environment and wanted to be part of it, not just a customer. When I voiced my desire to my parents, they responded, "Well, you'll have to ask Freddy." Freddy was the owner, a big man who looked grumpy all the time. But he would always graciously welcome the guests.

I'd often see him walk in his office with big stacks of cash. I thought to myself, *Man! I'm going to own a restaurant one day!* It seemed like a moneymaker to me at that age. My parents encouraged me to talk to Freddy, saying. "Ask him for a job and see what he says. It's worth a try. But you know, you can't get a work permit. You're too young."

I was undaunted. The next time he headed in our direction, I made sure he noticed me, shouting out even to my surprise, "Hey there, Mr. Freddy!" We made eye contact, and he favored me with a rare smile. "Well, hello there, young fella! What can I do for you?" I replied, "Well, I'd like to know if you have any jobs I could do to make money?"

He thought it over for a few seconds then answered, "Well, we could use you to bus tables. How old are you?" I was pretty sure he was going to shoot me down, but I grinned and said, "I'm thirteen, turning fourteen in nothing flat!" He looked me up and down, paused a bit, and then said, "Let's just have you start anyway." I was thrilled! I'm sure my parents were not happy at first, partly due to the fact that I had no transportation and it was too far to ride my bike.

Freddy worked out the details of bringing me on board. I'm sure he just paid me in cash under the table until I was old enough to work legally and receive a paycheck. I worked hard as a busboy and made great tips. I was successful in taking care of people because I made them feel like they belonged by treating them the way I wanted to be treated.

Freddy's was typically filled with business people and politicians. Regulars came in who had their usual tables. I got to know many of them, essentially the Who's Who of that area. Big-time hotshots in various fields would come in from Chicago. I got to see them connect every shift I worked, and observed how deals were made and networking was done. Because of this, I believed someone would open a door for me because I wasn't afraid of hard work. That was one of my earliest motivations. Every little opportunity people gave me fed that nourishment I had been yearning for all my life.

There was no shortage of odd jobs. If I needed to make money, I did everything I could to ingratiate myself to as many people as possible. Because of my tenacious attitude about work, I was regularly referred to people who needed everything from their lawns mowed to providing entertainment to their children for special occasions. I remember dressing up as the Easter Bunny in April, and then Santa Claus in December. I would get paid upwards of a hundred bucks, plus tips, to play with kids and entertain them for a few hours. That was easy money, and a lot of fun.

What I discovered was that whenever I needed a side gig for extra money, there was always somebody in the restaurant who could introduce me to someone who needed a job done. Because I was building quite a sizeable network even back then, I was also able to help many of my friends get some well-paying odd jobs.

School of Literal Hard Knocks

In high school, I was really into sports. Ours was a small, tough school where a lot of bad things went down. I was exposed to and experimented with drugs, which were more of an escape than anything else. I also got involved with a group of street kids who regularly used and sometimes sold drugs. I was a tough teenager who was always out and about, usually getting into trouble, fighting, and scrapping my way through.

Looking back, I realize I was fighting on another level, pushing to go somewhere else.

I even got stabbed a couple of times in scuffles, but never went to the hospital out of fear of getting those involved in more trouble. My mom found some bloody clothes I threw out after one of these incidents, but I told her it was just from a "par for the course" fight with someone. With my history of fighting, she didn't question it further.

Just like that little boy who'd run away from the house, my inner child was scared but still fighting to gain some level of significance. It's a core human need to be valued, to fit in. I was angry much of the time and usually didn't even know why. Much later in life, I discovered that the underlying deep hurt from my early years is what fueled a lot of that anger. My birth mother's abandonment of me was at the core of that. I got myself mixed up in some dicey scenes and tough places simply because I wanted so much to belong.

"Trouble" might as well have been my middle name. I was in a rough, dark space much of the time. Escape was my motive—escape from the pain of early onset rejection as well as being bullied, beaten up, and not fitting in. This deep hunger to get away from it all kept growing and gnawing at me. It hurt me, driving me into some negative situations, all born out of my desire to belong.

Even when I did feel like I belonged and was connected, I never allowed myself to be present and fully enjoy the moment. A part of me was always looking ahead. I bought into the "grass is always greener" philosophy at an extremely young age. I wanted to make sure that when that next better opportunity popped up, I'd be ready to grab it and never look back.

Bright Lights, Big City

In the fall of 1980, I started at Purdue University in Hammond. It was too close to my upbringing, and as a result, I stayed involved with everybody from my old neighborhood. I felt antsy and knew I needed a big change. This realization that I needed to move far away from my current personal network became crystal clear after one of my friends was killed by a rival gang member at a beach party. That happened right before my eyes, during one of our summer breaks.

I was still working at the restaurant while attending college. I connected with one of the regulars who was the president of the Chicago offices for Merrill Lynch. They were building out the technology infrastructure in the Chicago Board of Trade, as well as connecting all the securities exchanges online. For the first time, all the exchanges were being lit up and connected worldwide via an early private version of the internet. There he was in the world of high finance, and I was this teenager, just starting to dabble in computers.

Before long, I networked my way into helping him entertain by catering some parties at his house. One night while cleaning up after a bash there, I worked up the nerve to make another request. I cleared my throat, took a deep breath, and blurted out. "I'm wondering, what would it take for me to work with you and all those computers downtown in Chicago?" He stared right into my eyes for what seemed like minutes. Then he responded, "Dean, I really like you. You have a solid work ethic. I trust you. You can start in two weeks."

At that time, I was just a freshman at Purdue with a desire to own a restaurant one day. Next thing I knew, I was giving my two-week's notice at Freddy's. I need to give a nod to one of the guys back at the restaurant who said something I'll never forget: "No matter what you're doing, it doesn't matter if you're washing windows, if you're cutting grass—whatever it might be—just do the best job you possibly can. Somebody will discover that talent you have of being the best at whatever you do." I took those words of wisdom to heart, and whenever I took on a task or a job, I made sure I excelled at it.

I soon began working the midnight shift at the Board of Trade in downtown Chicago. To top it off, my boss put me in IBM School. I had made it—escaped my old neighborhood and its negative influences. The icing on the cake was that at the age of nineteen, I had an insanely amazing job. I started partying with some people at Merrill Lynch. This included going to bars, where I had no problem drinking because of the company I kept. Bartenders automatically assumed I was of age.

Meanwhile, back on the home front, my father kept himself busy as well. He was a supervisor at an engineering company on the trades side of things— very blue collar. He also sold Shaklee food supplements while going to night school. Dad eventually got his teaching degree and became a high school teacher at Lane Tech in Chicago.

He would often give me motivational cassette tapes, which I'd been listening to since about the age of fourteen. Sometimes he took me with him to motivational conferences. Once I met Zig Ziglar, who told me, "Hey, Kid! Remember, always help others get what they want, and you will always get what you want!"

I truly believe all of these positive influences saved my life. Even on this fast-paced journey, drinking and still occasionally doing drugs, there was always a nugget of sense in the back of my mind. Many times that inner voice would tell me *this is wrong.* Paying attention to it helped me make a few course corrections, mostly steering me away from what was familiar and comfortable.

One constant factor was my burning desire to get as far away as possible from my old life at that time. I was unsure whether I was running from the pain or running to the next best place of connection and safety. That's a question I didn't deal with until much later in my life.

It seemed like I had made a clean break from my negative past, but an entirely new set of problems and temptations arose while I worked at Merrill Lynch. It turned my worldview upside down and knocked the wind out of my sails for quite a while. More to come on that in an upcoming chapter, as well as the lessons it provided.

Whenever a Door Closes

Through no fault of my own, I wound up getting fired from Merrill Lynch due to my affiliation with my boss and his nefarious and downright corrupt actions. I was set up big-time when those now in power decided to completely clean house. It was like the rug had been pulled out from under me overnight. I felt confused, betrayed, and was next to broke.

There I was, two-and-a-half years into the corporate workforce, with just enough experience not to get hired. I was non-degreed and hadn't yet received my programming certification. I wanted to become a programmer because they were the ones making all the money back then.

I was faced with paying rent for my apartment in Rogers Park while barely subsisting on meager unemployment. I was still going to school. I'd been making damned good money, and this real life "riches-to-rags" story hit me all at once. No income, no severance pay. Needless to say, I was barely eking by.

Filing for and collecting unemployment was the most humiliating experience I'd ever gone through. It all but gave me an ulcer. My stomach hurt so much. I decided, "No matter what, I never ever want to have to do this again." It was yet another thing to move away from, and make sure it never happened in the future.

At school, there was a job bulletin board. I was willing to take anything that dealt with computers for any amount of money. One day, I saw a flier that read *Data Entry - $6.50 an hour.* I had been making $25 an hour at Merrill Lynch, so doing basic data entry for $6.50 was more than just a little step down. But I had learned the hard way that I was currently unemployable. All of the other jobseekers out there had at least three or four years of experience, plus a degree.

For me, it was similar to the movie *Groundhog Day.* I'd go in, ace the test, fly through the interview, but just couldn't get that job. Same scenario, over and over. The last network I had built up were now all fired and/or in jail. I had to start from scratch. My only network at the time included my roommates and my peeps at school, and that was about it. I was alone and had to drive myself to that next-best place. Again, was I running away from defeat and negativity, or towards my next self?

I pulled that notice off the job board and quickly was able set up an interview at the Children's Home and Aid Society in Chicago's Gold Coast. To my surprise, they immediately hired me to do data entry. I was grateful for the $6.50 an hour. It beat the heck out of unemployment. But, as usual, my mind was spinning, looking for the next opportunity to prove myself invaluable.

I never lost my belief that someday, someone would notice and give me a leg up. I also felt a connection to this nonprofit, as its mission was to help at-risk children who needed shelter as well as emotional and medical support. I had been one of those kids, so I deeply recognized how much good they were doing.

When I met Joan, the president of the organization, I said, "Thank you for this opportunity. But hey, this is my situation. I'm a new programmer. I'll do the data entry, but I also want to program for you for free." She raised an eyebrow, but I quickly continued, "What would you say to this ...as long as I do all my data entry work on time, I am willing to program in my free time at no charge. I can still go to my classes while I'm doing that."

Joan asked, "What's the catch, Dean? I'm sure you're aware that programmers average between $60 and $70 an hour." I absolutely was - that was my end game. I replied, "Well, that's the beauty of it. While I'm finishing up my degree, by doing your programming, I can use you as a reference." She smiled. "I'll help you in any way I can." Once again, I began to build my network in a new direction.

That hectic schedule became my life over the next few months. I was just scraping by. If you've ever gone through lean times, you will appreciate this. I was living on about three cans of tuna and a box of crackers per week, with the occasional mac and cheese.

After a few months, Joan called me into her office: "Dean, I want you to meet someone." She proceeded to introduce me to a woman who worked on the other side as a programmer. I'll never forget shaking hands with her. She said, "I'm the programmer here. You've been writing some code, and you're doing a really good job."

I thought, *Oh, so you're the one that I've been writing this code for*. We chit-chatted a bit and then she shared that her husband was an IBM repairman. He had just heard that Midland-Ross Corporation, a huge steel company in Cicero, needed someone to write a payroll system in COBOL.

It so happened I could write in COBOL like nobody's business. I was learning some other computer languages, but still didn't have my certification. She continued, "It only pays $20 an hour, but you can get 40 hours a week." My eyes about popped out of my head as a big grin spread across my face. "That's more than fine! It's a helluva lot more than six bucks an hour!"

The stars seemed to be aligning for me once again. My networking was paying off. That was the same week I received my programming certification. This new opportunity was the best graduation present I could have hoped for.

From this networked opportunity I created my first startup. From there I was able to build a wide variety of opportunities that I'll share more about throughout this book. This will allow you to see how you, too, can continuously build vibrant networks of support and exchange. At this juncture, though, rather than another

Back to the Future story, I'll share a back-to-the-present one.

Here and Now

Social Jack™, the company I founded, was created to help top professionals and entrepreneurs build their digital business influence. My team and I have served over 100,000 influencers. We offer both live and online training through our custom-designed social-networking platform. It provides a social media learning resource that people can tap into 24/7.

We also offer turnkey packages. Our company is built on a learning and networking foundation. To this end, we not only help our clients learn how to best organize and leverage the power of social media, but we go further by assisting them in making vibrant, sustainable connections.

The foundation for all of this was based on my daily observation of the clientele at Freddy's Steakhouse, way back in the day. As that young busboy, I started listening and learning from my boss and coworkers, and asking a lot of questions. This predated the internet and social media boom by a few decades. But I was fortunate even then to learn the ropes and the value of networking, of building a network of trusted connections. When social media cropped up, it felt like a natural evolution to transfer what I had learned and mastered over two decades.

Along my path, I realized how valuable it is to connect with people. You must invest time and focus on creating, nurturing, and continuously cultivating long-lasting, mutually beneficial relationships. It's vital to be consistently present with those in your network. I also realized how important it is be present in your hurt and pain, your joy and sadness—whatever it is—to be with those emotions and with those people. This reveals authenticity, which builds trust.

As relationships are forged, you create the groundwork to build a solid networking team with those who are on that journey with you—from that point to the next. You take people with you as you move up the success scale.

FIRST *STEPS*
to Influence

Start with a Beginner's Mindset: *FIRST* Thoughts

Even though I've always felt that I had a beginner's mindset, it took me a while to generate results from that vantage point. One of the things I've come to believe is that in order for someone to tell their truth, they must:

- Be authentic and transparent.
- Truly want to attract, connect, and be in a relationship with others.
- Know and believe they are okay just as they are.

To do these things, a beginner's mindset is a requisite. All beginners have to deal with a lot of pain and discomfort. That's just how learning, growth, and development work. I know this from personal experience, believe me. In fact, when I was rereading the introduction to this book, it brought up a lot of pain. In the interest of practicing what I preach, I'm going to be completely honest with you about that. I literally wept for almost half a day due to the pain that I felt.

A lot of people want to create influence and generate results, although they're not always willing to change and transform. I know that's the biggest thing that stood in my way, as it does for many people.

I was brought up to "be a good boy." So for people to think you were good, you needed to look and act good, to toe the line: *Don't cry. Be a man.* These are all early behavioral patterns that we're groomed to develop. Because these guidelines are deeply instilled during childhood, I believe many adults are still wired that way. We're not wired to believe that it's okay to tell the truth and be wrong, or to look at your wrongs and admit you need the help of others.

However, the minute you do that, you begin to grow your network and connect more deeply with others so that they feel free to exchange more deeply with you. In other words, take the lead in creating an environment of trust, connection, and plenty of opportunities for both of you to evolve. I am truly amazed by the magic this provides to this day.

If you want to be an influencer, here's the most important personal thing to take to heart: you seriously need to say you're willing to change. Period. This led me to embrace my fear of being wrong. It has helped me stay open to change, and to know that it's okay to be raw, to be the "real you." I've discovered that doing so gives other people comfort and lets them genuinely connect with you.

Pretty much everyone I meet has something that they have tried to hide. They feel like they'll be shamed in some way if they share it. Being willing to be raw could be the richest part of the process. You can absolutely count on the fact that someone—many people—will be touched by that realness. So be willing to get real and raw. You will also begin to trust yourself, and therefore trust others more.

I do feel that it is essential for people to get raw and honest with each other, and to expose themselves. In other words, it's time to get naked. Don't be shocked. Relax. This isn't about taking your clothes off. It's about being authentic, and being transparent about what's going on. Not being afraid to share how you truly feel.

When I first started exploring this track, I was thinking about two things about business advisors who have the most colorful, effective networks. First, of course, they all had a beginner's mindset. Second, they all understand that you must get real before you can get successful.

What's interesting about this is that when I was told to bring some of our business advisors together, we conducted a social experiment. I was blown away by the results. This involved two people I truly respect and admire, Barry Goodman and Tom Meyer. I said, "These are two powerful businessmen, both trusted advisors and colleagues I know I can say anything to, and, in turn, they can say anything to me. We have a solid relationship because we three have these truth-telling conversations regularly."

I pondered, "What would it be like if we had a networking event where people were able to get raw and honest, and talk about the things that are good and turned out great, as well as about the mistakes they've made? What if this event was a place where they would be able to admit those mistakes? A place where they could come through as being authentic— and *still* be a trusted business advisor?"

I've found that we can build trust in a shorter amount of time when we are honest in front of one another. You can take that model and convert it to exchange business referrals at a faster level. It speeds things up because we not only know you do good work, but we also realize you're a good person.

So BARE Networking was born, which stands for Business Advisor Referral Exchange. That acronym means being bare in front of the room and with each other. But it's not just an acronym. It has meaning. We're basically getting naked with each other emotionally and psychologically.

We tested that social experiment and, from it, created our first BARE Networking event. We set a limit of fifty people. Within eight days, we had sixty people on our waiting list.

To ensure the event was a professional and safe place, the requirement was that you had to know one of the hosts. I didn't want to make it too big. I wanted to keep it intimate enough to ensure that it was as powerful as I believed it to be—an environment where trusted faith would be nurtured. Now that the first event was successful, I have a foundation on which future meetings can be built.

Power Move: *Write yourself a commitment letter.*

Write a commitment letter to yourself. Be honest while doing this. Be sure to include all the *whys—why* it's important, *why* you need to change, *why* you need to have a beginner's mindset. You also need to realize who else you are doing it for.

First and foremost, do it for yourself. You might have some other grounding elements that factor into your letter. For example, there may be significant people within your life whom you believe drive you to do it collectively. But first, do it for yourself. Commit to yourself. Many people don't want to do that.

You may also want to post your letter someplace prominent in your home, where it will be front and center in your consciousness at the beginning of each day. This may mean putting it on your bathroom mirror, as this location helps set the tone for your morning. You may also find it helpful to put it on your phone, since we refer to our phones so often in our daily lives. Another good idea would be to "snail mail" the note to yourself. This last strategy has worked well for me.

Also consider creating a vision board. I have one at home that contains many of the Power Moves I share within this book. Choose whatever venues you absolutely know you will notice daily. Include the Power Moves that speak to you, and integrate them into your daily routine. I promise doing this will strengthen and motivate you.

Want to be *FIRST*

I've been labeled a *people pleaser:* someone who goes out of their way to make sure everyone is taken care of and happy. After years of going down that path, I now realize I don't have to take on that role to build relationships with others. Neither should you.

This *people pleasing addiction* is incredibly powerful. For most of us, it's also the most difficult, challenging aspect of becoming a business influencer. How something so simple can be so frightening and hard to overcome tells me that releasing it is a critical step in becoming who we have the potential to be. I promise, once you let it go, you'll feel amazingly empowered.

What do I mean about "wanting to be *FIRST?*" It means that, within your network, you'll come to realize that everybody has a desire to be wanted, to be needed, to be *FIRST.* Putting oneself, one's needs, wants, desires, and financial future ahead of everyone else is not okay for a lot of people. They balk, hesitate, or refuse this concept in part, or entirely, based on their belief system and how they were raised.

Even though it's a core human need to have significance—to be known and wanted—some of us struggle with this aspect of ourselves. The reality is we need people to need us—especially to think of us and reach out to us *first.*

For me, the need to be wanted and to be thought of first stems from my own early childhood development.

Through my experiences, struggling as a young kid who spent more time on the streets than at home, I often felt unwanted. In my professional life, however, I have learned most of us have a core desire to be thought of as *first*. Further, this desire is an integral part of achieving success in your business life.

This is a big deal—for people to not just want to be first but to act on that intention and say, "Hey! I'm okay. I'm a good person. I'm not perfect, but I'm a good person. It's okay for me to be first. It's okay for me to say *no* to things; to turn down people and requests that don't advance me toward my goals and needs. I want to convert my desires into actions and success, and that's okay."

When we're not honest with ourselves, we're also unable to be honest with others. We hold ourselves back from being *first*. If we refuse to be authentic, then we don't build trust with others. Our network doesn't trust us because we don't trust ourselves. It's a vicious cycle, but I have faith in you. You can break it.

I've been at that point where I didn't trust myself, especially in the early days. I didn't trust that I was making sound decisions, that I was a good person— none of that. It took me a long time to come to the realization that I'm okay. I'm not perfect. I make mistakes. I'm human. I just had to arrive at that point. To do that, I still had to peel that back and again get honest with myself before I could be okay with being *first* in my life as well as in the lives of others.

To this day, I still must watch this, this willingness to accept that it's okay that I want to be *first*. I want to be the first person people think of when they want to become a business influencer (be known). I want to be first in their minds when they want to build the very best community around them. Up front and first in their minds whenever they want to be connected and generate relationships to increase referrals.

I want to be the *first* one people think of. Yet there are times where I feel like I can't just be me. I have to perform; I have to work super hard. In fact, when I first met my friend, Melissa G. Wilson, after we talked for a while, she said, "You're the hardest working man in show business!" That has stuck with me ever since.

I wondered, "Why is that?" I concluded that it's my desire to be *first,* but not believing I'm enough—just as I am—that moves me into honestly assessing my limiting beliefs. I'm certainly not alone when it comes to having subscribed to a set of limiting beliefs. I want to quickly share how one mega-successful celebrity describes her adoption of those limiting beliefs.

Oprah was a People Pleaser. Are You?

At a recent presentation, Oprah Winfrey opened her keynote speech by saying, "I had the disease of pleasing people." Let that soak in for a minute. I'm pretty sure it will hit home with you. It might quite possibly be a shock and a wake-up call. In her presentation, she shared that her own journey paralleled the journey of *The Oprah Winfrey Show*.

In the early days of her talk show, much like many of us in our early twenties, Oprah was basically just happy to have a job. During those initial years, her producers made most of her decisions for her. They even invited white nationalists to be guests on one episode.

As it turned out, that episode shifted everything. From that day forward, Oprah confronted her producers and demanded that they allow her to decide who appeared on the show. This wasn't because those guests made her feel targeted and uncomfortable. It was because she realized her show had provided them a platform to spread hatred and negativity out into the world.

That pivotal episode was the dawning of her realization that her purpose in life was to elevate people. That included using the vehicle of her show as a force only for good. Simply taking her show in that direction to achieve her purpose was not enough. Are you a people pleaser now? Have you ever been? If so, you know how difficult it is to refuse to take on that role, even for Oprah.

The biggest hurdle for people pleasers is struggling with their guilt—the guilt that results after you have incorporated "no" into your vocabulary. This doesn't resolve itself overnight. In her speech, Oprah admitted to dealing with this guilt for years, right up until the time she read Gary Zukav's book, *The Seat of the Soul*. It opened her eyes to the fact that the energy driving what you say and the way you say it has power. This shifted everything for her.

For instance, when asked for a favor that you do not wish to do, the typical people pleaser will agree and just do it anyway. You might try to rationalize it by feeling good because you put your friend's needs ahead of your own. But by doing that, you're infusing your decision with negative feelings, which in turn causes you to transmit negative energy, and to feel resentment about your choices. Since that's the end result, why bother to do it in the first place?

Power Move: *Write down five reasons why you want to be first.*

Figure out five big reasons or *whys* that you want to be *first*, and then write those down. Don't skip this. It's important to capture this stuff in writing. It helps bring your thoughts into tangible 3D form. We're living in a 3D world, right? Harnessing your thoughts and writing them down helps you feel more empowered and on track. It helps you manifest things you desire rather than passively having the thoughts randomly run through your mind. It's also a form of self discipline that will guide you to where you wish to be.

FIRST be Honest about Your Limiting Beliefs

Be honest about the fact that you have limiting beliefs. We all have them. This means you need to just sit there and own that fact. This allows you to say, "I'm okay, but I'm also *[fill in the blank]*." As a child, I was told, "Be good and don't cry." This, combined with many other things, affected me as a person. I was motivated to be good for everybody else around me, rather than doing what was best for me.

I believe this is inherently an area people need to explore. If you're afraid of putting yourself *first* or telling your stories, there's a reason for that. You have to get honest. What's real? What are the limiting beliefs preventing you from being successful? What's keeping you from going to the next level? What's keeping you from telling the truth? We have limiting beliefs within ourselves, and if we don't conquer them, we are basically setting the stage to bullshit ourselves.

We tell ourselves that it's not okay to tell people certain things. In my own experience, that includes revealing things like turning to drugs when I was younger. Feeling that it's not okay to tell people that I was in street fights, and was stabbed. Part of us wants to hide those things away, because It's not okay to share these things because people will think badly of you. Don't reveal that you learned about death the hard way at a young age because you had so many friends who were victims of suicide, murder, and circumstances. These types of revelations may be hard for some people to hear, but it's totally okay to share those experiences.

Your left brain balks at being so forthcoming. Your inner dialogue insists, "It's not okay to tell people that when the market bombed out, you probably could have done things to prevent your own downfall. Instead, you lost your whole net worth, including your home, your cars, and everything else. It's not okay to reveal that you bottomed out and felt like a failure. It's not okay to say that because people will think poorly of you."

(This all happened to me and I'll share more about it later)

Those are some of my personal limiting beliefs that helped me conclude that people need to get true and honest with themselves. There are all kinds of different programs and methods to support you in this. I've been through all the motivational speakers and programs, including Tony Robbins, Zig Ziglar, Dale Carnegie—you name it. You'll find that most of my recommended reading/listening list includes tons of motivational books. What led me to absorb them was the fact that I believed that I was never enough, and that I always had to be better.

Power Move: *Be honest about your limiting beliefs and inventory them.*

Create an inventory of your limiting beliefs. Right now. This is for your eyes only, so don't hold back. Write down what you currently believe and give examples of how these beliefs appear in your life. More detail is better to help you connect deeply with each belief in the moment. Examples may include things you currently say you can't do, or things that you currently do that you know you don't have to do.

You'll recognize something is preventing you from taking a different path. You'll know that you're ready to change, and release all limiting beliefs in your life that prevent you from advancing.

When I was reading the book Transformed! by Bob and Judith Wright, it hit me that it was undeniably important for me to get to a bottom line level of my fear. They refer to this process as "Name It to Tame It." If there's anything scaring you, make an inventory of your limiting beliefs behind your fears. Be honest with yourself. First, write down what you currently believe. Then write what's actually true. You may very likely find out your fears are not as ominous as you've thought them to be.

If your limiting beliefs come up regularly you might want to think of them like weeds. When you're growing your "garden of beliefs," note that "you can't seed if you don't first weed." So it makes a lot of sense to weed regularly. Regularly weed out your beliefs that are blocking your path to success. This will require a raw and honest effort.

You can't simply wish them away with positive thinking or mantras like, "There's no weeds, no weeds, no weeds." Trust me, there are weeds! I encourage you to be a diligent gardener. If you are, your garden of beliefs will stay a thing of beauty.

Fear of Success

This is more common than you might imagine. Many people don't realize it when they experience a fear of success. They may not even know there is such a thing. Several of my clients are Fortune 500 success stories. In many cases, they're overachievers or extremely high-level achievers. They're industry thought leaders. Yet

during their long journey to that echelon, I find that they don't know how to pinpoint fear of success, or don't understand what it is.

I associate this fear with not wanting to look bad. There have been times when I've been on a route to success in generating additional business. Fear of success becomes stifling because I don't want to mess anything up. Over time, I've learned to embrace it and say, "Oh, wait, this is an opportunity to determine how to scale this." In the past, my knee-jerk reaction was to thwart my own success by saying, "Let's just slow down here and not grow so much until we can figure this out." However, that is what's called operating from scarcity.

On the one hand, you have the abundance mindset that says, "I'm generating a ton of appointments and business here." But with the next breath, you find yourself feeling overwhelmed, like you're going to mess up somehow. A better solution is to ask yourself, "How can we handle more of this type of business and also make it profitable?" There's a balance there that I've experienced firsthand, as well as observed many of my clients going through that process.

For instance, recently my team and I were in a board meeting with one of our banking clients. They raised the following concern, "Well, we don't want too much business as we believe we might not be able to handle it all." We probed deeper to get to the core of their concerns which we discovered centered on their fear that particular types of business would not be profitable. Through our process of focused probing we helped them come to the realization that they could handle a business upswing and effectively manage any opportunities that were not going to be profitable.

I give this example to demonstrate that there are many reasons why the fear of success comes up, especially in an organizational environment. But it also lies within you. If left unchecked, you can sabotage your own efforts.

Let's jump into getting past those fears right now.

Set Your *FIRST* Goals

You need to understand that there's a reason you're reading this book. There's a reason you want influence. There's a reason you have a core need to be significant. You were born with it. It's okay! Your goals may be as straightforward as, "I want to be a thought leader in my industry," or "I want to get promoted or generate more income." It could be "I need to get twenty times my sales quota from the prior year." Maybe it's, "I want to build and sell my business within three years."

Whenever I'm working with people doing goal setting, we always create our BHAG (Big Hairy Audacious Goal) goals. Part of our men's weeklong leadership program at www.wrightfoundation.org includes coming up with our BHAGs. We come up with our short-term goals that are going to get us to that bigger goal. This sets the tone for our entire year. It's interesting that sometimes what you think are your goals are not the ones that will get you to your next level of success.

The first thing to do is make sure that you set the goals that you know are going to help you move your *success needle*. For example, as I'm writing this chapter, I'm planning out my next year. I have a certain number of business goals that must be in place to hit certain numbers, so my business can reach a certain value. This involves raising additional capital so that we can grow the business.

We do this (and you should, too) in order to have a strong exit, or to create a space where everybody in the company is taken care of. At the end of the BHAGs, there must be goals along the way that are realistic for you to achieve.

Right now, one of my personal BHAGs is to lose 20 pounds. When doing this, I'm not going to just write down my three goals and then lose 20 pounds. Wouldn't that be great? But there's always more to it than that. When setting your first goals, make sure that you are dividing them into categories. I learned an excellent system created by Anthony Robbins in his *Time of Your Life: Three Steps to Take Control of Your Life*.

His system involves transforming your everyday stress and anxiety into drive and fulfillment to create a life of your *choosing* rather than a life of *reaction*. Tony calls it a Rapid Planning Method (RPM) and says it's "...a revolutionary breakthrough in life management that focuses on what matters most to you in your life." This was one of my earliest and most successful time-tracking systems, and I highly recommend it.

One of the things we always did was put our life into categories. We had business and personal categories for goals. A word of caution: you want to make sure this doesn't get overwhelming.

The purpose of this book centers around building business influence. One of your primary steps toward doing that is to figure out *why* you're doing this. Do you want to be a thought leader? Are you looking to increase business or sales? Do you want to become a motivational speaker? Do you want to become an author and work with Melissa Wilson on writing and publishing your book? What are the goals that are going to transform you into that influencer you've always known you could be?

It's important to ask, "Who are you going to be in partnership with to make sure you achieve your goals, and in turn help them achieve their goals?" There should be some mutuality in this when you create partnerships. Because I'm working on getting healthier, I've reached out to some folks who are supporting that goal by holding me accountable. They're like diet and exercise check-in buddies.

I've worked regularly with CEO's that are good at accountability. I must give a quick shout out to Frank Montro and Brian Kuzdas. We check in with each other often so that we stay on our goal to lose weight by eating healthy and exercising. We each track our success through a mobile app.

Additionally, I talk with my fitness trainer, Darin Steen, on a regular basis. He's my main motivator, who's also part of that success plan. (You will read more about Darin in Chapter 2.)

I can't emphasize this next part enough: Don't go after your goals all by yourself; this book isn't about being alone. In fact, it's the furthest thing from it. Remember, I grew up feeling alone on the streets. Today, I am adamant about nobody being left behind, nobody doing this alone. Nobody should ever have to feel alone in this world. I am committed to making sure that everything you do, you're doing it with someone in mind. You're partnering with someone and/or building a team from this point forward. That's a huge part of your goal.

Power Move: *Make a list of the goals you want to achieve.*

When featured in Steve Olsher's Book, *Internet Prophets,* I went on the book tour with him. He would introduce me as the ultimate connector, saying that my system was like a Social GPS. I always liked that reference, as my systems, including this one, have you:

1. Commit to a destination (goal)
2. Clarify your current position (your story/ network), then
3. Take the necessary roads and turns to arrive at your destination (goal).

This is how I always viewed this. I just never realized that it could be summarized by the simple reference of a Social GPS.

This is your first Power Move, and it's a big one. If you don't write it down, from my perspective, it doesn't count. Don't just write out your goals. Make sure that you place timeframes on them and attach numbers to each one.

For example, if you have sales goals, you need to create goals around how many appointments you need to get X number of proposals, which in turn will lead to X number of deals. Be absolutely clear about the numbers and dates that you're going to achieve things by:

- Creating a clear list of both your short-term and long-term goals.
- Dreaming big! Don't be afraid to dream big. Make sure you have a Big Hairy Audacious Goal (BHAG). You deserve this and more!
- Putting hard dates and numbers as to your outcomes and goals. Next, make sure you include people that can help you get there so you're not alone at the finish line.

DEVELOP YOUR *FIRST IDEAL TARGETS*

This is all about clearly communicating with those who are helping you on your journey to influence. When you look at generating leads, who are your first targets for customers and/or partners? For example, let's say that you're in business development. You're a business-to-business (B2B) practitioner. You're a business-management consultant who helps mid-market companies transition or sell their businesses. Who are your ideal customers in this adventure?

For the sake of this exercise, let's say the targets are companies ranging from $2 million to $10 million in size. That means the ideal customers are the CEO or C-Suite executives of those organizations that you need to reach. Those are the ideal people who can help your business get to the numbers that you've articulated in your goals. You know that not only do you need those people, but you also need a good solid business team behind you (and some good partners).

Let's take it to the next step. What does the ideal partner look like? In this adventure, they might look like attorneys who work with large organizations. Maybe they're accountants or insurance professionals or bankers who work with those size companies. What you're doing now is starting to assemble a team or at least specific ideal targets of people you want to talk to.

It's vital that you do this. In today's world, especially when we go digital, it feels as though there are far too many people that we could reach, including those that might become connections. It gets to the point where there are so many people that we just cannot make a choice. It's overwhelming, and it's hard to work with. If you're not specific, the enormity of it can freeze you in your tracks. By defining your ideal targets and partners, you're positioning yourself to be on a smoother road to success.

In fact, we often find that people either connect to everyone and never or rarely engage effectively, or they connect with too few and assemble the wrong team. Either way, it's inefficient. Make sure that you can clearly identify those targets who are both people you want to work with as clients or customers, as well as partners in the world.

Power Move: *Pinpoint as specifically as possible everything about your targets.*

Once you've identified your targets and their positions in industry or certain market segments, review that. Pinpoint as many details as possible. Is there a certain geography involved? Make sure you can clearly document those details. Don't necessarily put this in your own inimitable jargon, but write it using clear, concise language someone else can understand.

Why is this important? Because when you come to me seeking help in generating a referral, or you want to grow your business career—whatever that looks like for you—the first thing I'm going to ask you is "Exactly who are you looking for?" That's what everyone should ask you. Be able to easily and clearly state your response.

Whether you're at a networking event, on LinkedIn, Twitter, or anywhere on the internet, you should be able to clearly see who that ideal target is. As we move and talk about ways to do this digitally and online, we always say, "Pretend you're looking at your ideal client." We'd like you to have a picture or a name, or somebody you know who makes you say, "Man! If I could have more clients like so-and-so...." List that person.

We even have our clients put a picture of that client on their desk (or in front of them somewhere) so they visualize *that's* who they're going for. More connections that are similar to that person. You might joke, "Well, of course, it's clients who pay well!" or who have certain characteristics. But most importantly, you must visualize what that ideal target or customer looks like, as well as identifying what ideal partner(s) can help you reach them.

Personal Branding:
Put Yourself *FIRST*

Part of our Influencer Development program at Social Jack includes an intake process with our clients. Initially we get them to answer questions, and then we get them into a flow. The important thing is for them to find their voice. That happens as they relax and almost unconsciously tell us their story. In most cases, we get clients who believe they know where they're going when they first begin working with us. But then they discover they're uncertain. That's when their story begins to get a bit fuzzy.

Colin Egglesfield, a television and film star, relocated from Los Angeles back to his roots in Chicago. He just knew it was time for that. But he's still acting in Hollywood movies (at the time of this book). He was in a recent movie with Sylvester Stallone, *Backtrace,* and another one with Kate Hudson. He has a long track record of TV appearances, including extended runs on *All My Children* and *Rizzoli & Isles*. He's had a very successful career.

When I met him, he wanted to transition into more of his "steady income" business—real estate. Essentially, he wanted to be two different people, a Hollywood actor and a real estate guy. As we dug deeper into his story, we discovered we could blend both.

By going into more depth with him—as happens with everybody who goes through our program—we found out that there was a part of his story he was afraid to tell. With Colin, it was that he's a cancer survivor. He was uncertain about wanting that known for a number of reasons. First of all, it's really scary and brings up a lot of bad memories.

I could definitely relate. Just as I share in this book, some of my own memories contain parts of me that I don't want people to know. But in my work with my team at my business, we have learned that when we get real with our stories and dive into our feelings with our story where people can connect to us emotionally, that's where all the magic happens.

We're now talking about this in public, helping Colin move into his next true self, and it's magical stuff. When people find out such personal details, they look at him differently and say, "Oh, you're human, you're real. You're not just some successful actor whose life is a bed of roses and nothing has ever gone wrong for you." They connect with him on a totally new level and feel a new sense of warmth towards him.

We're all human, and the minute we start unveiling this, it transforms into sheer magic. By working with him, we started to see that he was okay with weaving that into his story. To learn more about Colin, check out his own book, *Agile Artist.*

A New Chicago Digital Business Influencer

Frank Montro is another Chicagoan who is an extremely positive, motivational person. He posts on social media constantly. He's a client of ours that sometimes posts so much it's tough for us to get the thought leadership stuff out there. But we love his level of energy and motivation, and he always gets a response.

In fact, he just got rated the Number 1 realtor on social media in Chicago.

This is huge, considering what a big city Chicago is. Frank was in the Top 10 last year, but now he's rocking it even more. So we blended his personality with his business. Frank is a natural leader. Now with the help of social media, he can lead even more proactively.

He is building and rebuilding neighborhoods in Chicago and helping families. Many times, he works with investors as he goes into some of the depressed neighborhoods in Chicago, mostly throughout the south side. He finds blocks where there's an opportunity to help a lot of people, or a neighborhood that needs a major uplift.

Along with his investors, he buys homes that are available and makes them look gorgeous. I don't know how he does it, but somehow, he manages to keep the homes affordable. He's committed to helping every single family that's getting into a home, even if they need credit repair to do so.

This side of his story was not being told, so I insisted, "Frank, yes! You have investors, but you need to also tell your network how you and your investors are changing hundreds of families' lives each year." He's been helping these families for at least a decade, and he has not only changed the lives of neighborhoods, he has changed an entire city.

One day I told him, "Frank, you're more than a mover and a shaker. You are positively helping all these families." Once he got real with the bigger story of his life, he realized, "Wow, yeah—that's who I am!" So right away he jumped onto his LinkedIn account and other social media to start telling this part of his story.

It's a common human experience that people are afraid to talk about the good that they do. They feel like they're bragging or boasting, but it's not that. It's letting people know that you care, and that, damn it, you're going to do this whether they like it or not. This is who you are, and this is why you're doing it.

One beautiful thing about telling your *deeper story* is that, from there, you can move into that part of you where, for whatever reason, your limiting beliefs are holding you back. I love the rich, authentic stories that emerge when we interview our clients. They share, but will often put the brakes on in places, saying something like, "But I don't want to talk about ... *that.*"

That's when we dig deeper. That's when the magic happens. These deeper stories help reveal their vulnerability and, as a result, create a more compelling and engaging story that truly connects with others.

This is where people start to find their richer identity. From there, we get down to storytelling, sharing someone's unique journey in life. We help our clients unmask those vulnerable parts of themselves so that they float to the surface where they can be seen as rich lessons for others, which, in turn, frees them to be all they can be. We've seen amazing shifts in leaders who share their journeys in this way.

Darin Steen Reveals Truth

I've known Darin Steen for about ten years. He's an amazing fitness guy. He just won a contest with Arnold Schwarzenegger, and he's trained Dr. Mercola and his family for several years. He even had a prince from Saudi Arabia fly his son into Chicago for him to train. He'll be training Tony Romo, the retired Dallas Cowboys' quarterback.

Darin is such a caring, beautiful person. Many celebrities suffer from trying to keep up with their "image." Darin helped me realize that it's incredibly tough on them. They need to constantly commit to working out to stay in their best shape to maintain their image. But they are so much more than that. They feel they need to have a tough outer image. Yet this isn't their authentic self.

I can relate to Darin for several reasons. For instance, he often uses humor to mask his emotions. He's training me right now, and I'm learning a lot from him on multiple levels.

He often uses his training techniques and his toughness to mask the hurt and softness inside of him. He has had a tough life, losing his father early on. Then taking on the care of his mom was added to his plate, and later, being a single dad raising two daughters. Growing up, his life was extremely blue collar, and he had to get by on very little money. At a young age, he discovered within himself that he had the ability to grab hold of driving urges and see them through. This took him to the next part of himself.

When I started working with Darin, he revealed that he suffered from severe bouts of depression. In a recent conversation with him, he shared his desire to train top CEOs and executives to help them address their depression issues.

He stated, "I know they (CEOs) have so much responsibility and pressure that they often feel depressed. Because I've been there, I want to be sensitive that they may be on the brink of either going into full blown depression, or even so far as to commit suicide. They're terrified of reaching a point of just crumbling in front of everybody because the pressure is so high. And most of them don't easily or willingly reveal this part of themselves."

He added, "I feel for them. I connect to them, and want them to be in their peak condition and topmost shape. Not just their bodies, but mind and soul, too. Not being confident about themselves is another thing on that list, but I also want to be there mentally with them in the workout." He effectively combines mental fitness with mental toughness while improving their physical strength.

As I'm training with him, he's helping me work through goal setting and the *whys* behind my training with him—*why* I want to be in peak shape. As he revealed that he knows most people feel pressure and are afraid to talk about it—when it comes to the surface, he's witnessed that it helps drive them to that next level of best self. He always says, "Make the rest of your life the best of your life." Every time you step in to work with him, you're stepping into this new doorway and window of who your next best self can be.

I believe that once he gets even more comfortable with this part of his story and giving talks in that way, he'll be unstoppable. When he's on his game, his confidence level is just through the roof. But when he's feeling down and not altogether himself, he can keep getting pulled back to what I call the "dark side." I'm working with him so that he knows that his social team is always with him and he's not alone.

I think when people have a hard time going to that dark spot of their story, the biggest factor is that they feel isolated, alone. They might be ashamed. They simply don't feel as powerful. They feel they must wear this persona because they're the person everybody needs to go to.

One of the beautiful aspects of Darin is when he gets to that part of his real self, people are just going to line up. He's already trained thousands of people. That's not what I'm talking about.

I believe he will be overwhelmed with requests for more than training. He has the ability to inspire many people. I can see him doing a TED talk, possibly writing his own book and giving keynote speeches. I am so excited to watch him soar through his transformation by revealing the tough truth about himself. I know it will lead to even greater things for him.

On a personal note, as my skill set expanded and my career evolved to include more facets, my own branding started to become a bit confusing. I was previously associated with the fields of telecommunication, ERP, and CRM. But once I began immersing myself into working on social media, a new spin occurred that surprised me.

I chose to become an expert on LinkedIn because I saw its potential for building business influence before anybody else knew what it had to offer in that arena. Suddenly people started saying, "Oh, yeah - Dean? He's the LinkedIn guy." Although that was flattering on one hand, on the other, I didn't want to be typecast or tied to a single product or platform. Rather, my desire for my brand is that I am thought of as a discerning connector—the guy who helps thought leaders build their unique brand and support networks online, assisting them in becoming thought of *first* in their respective fields.

FIRST Find Your Voice, Tell The Truth

Rather than merely a shift, I'm seeing a metamorphosis in the business world today. In my case, I started implementing this change by going into huge companies like GE. I built relationships inside these companies, and discovered so many of the people there were hiding a lot of their personal truth.

They bought into the belief that not only must they prevent themselves from appearing weak or vulnerable (because the company would look down upon them), but feared that if they revealed that part of themselves, they wouldn't be a suitable candidate for the job.

One big challenge with social media is that people assume that others are completely on top of their game and totally together. They're obviously successful, so everything must be absolutely perfect with them. But often, they're not who they appear to be. I think it's created this "it's okay to have this false self out there" ethos. We've done it enough through most of our lives that we're conditioned to have it out there. It's tough for people to find their real voice. We take them through an exercise and ask them some critical questions.

What became apparent to me was that if they don't speak the truth to the companies with whom they work, these people can't grow their relationships to their fullest potential. There are many people holding back their own personal and/or company truths. Because of this reality, I committed myself to create a culture at my company where we focus daily on building a human brand.

Pick Yourself Up, Dust Yourself Off, Start All Over....

I'll give you an example of a personal situation from my past that was hard to talk about for many years. In my mid-20s, I was in constant motion, always connecting, networking, and never forgetting the value of those skills. I was one of the fastest programmers around. The only reason I stopped programming was because I'm a people person.

I couldn't stand being cooped up with machines for eight hours a day and not interacting with people. I became a systems analyst and a systems architect— not by degree, but by choice. I studied hard, took extra classes, went to the library, and read all the books on the topic. I started designing systems and databases.

I bought a 1,000-square-foot condo in the Hyde Park area, left the CPA firm where I'd been working, and started my next business out of my new home on Lakeshore Drive. At that time, restaurant inventory management systems were emerging. I became one of the go-to people for accounting packages.

In February 1989, I met a wonderful girl named Holly, and we started dating. We got married in 1992. When 1994 rolled around, I started a computer software/ hardware consulting company. Life was good!

One of the big beef families at that time in Chicago was Buona Beef. I got connected to the Buona Beef family, to the Turanos, and others who were on the move. Déjà vu struck me, as I again found myself involved in the restaurant business. This became another new connection source as I worked my way into the whole network of the Italian food industry. I was helping them expand and develop all that new technology.

I can remember the first time I went to the Buona's sprawling 4,000-plus square foot behemoth bungalow. It was breathtaking, finished to the nines, top to bottom. With two kitchens, six bedrooms, and four baths, it was massive and beautiful. We expanded two of the connected bedrooms into one. That became our new office. Suddenly, we were all getting super successful. I began to take on investors to build up my first dot com, which was an online B2B— a university that I started. I felt unstoppable.

I was making friends with all these major players, eating at the best restaurants, partying, driving nice cars, and taking my life to that next level. Then the Buona's decided they wanted to move to Burr Ridge. Thanks to them, I had the confidence to say, "Well, I want this house." (The 4,000+ foot stunner.)

I was making enough money, and with their help financing it, I figured out how to buy that incredibly lovely home. At that time, it was just me and Holly in this gigantic house! There we were, living in this gorgeous showplace, which is one of the nicest houses in that area to this day. Everything was amazingly positive, and it felt like it would just keep getting better.

We continued building the business up. I found myself hiring more people and getting some investors. The market was going like gangbusters. We got the whole company up to about $100 million valuation. On paper, I was worth close to $47 million. We were just rocking it—hard! This was a brand new world for me, far from where I started.

Then *BOOM*. In the mid-2000s, the market started to take a shit. Everything was crazy. I was just a little too full of myself to listen to people. An associate wanted to be my business coach, but I arrogantly blew him off by saying, "Really? You're not successful. What could you possibly tell me?" There was this cocky part of me that often comes with getting too successful, too young.

The market faltered some more and then tanked in an unstoppable downward spiral. I had big contracts pending, and we were also building call centers and doing telecommunication, complete with all the software and programming. All kinds of cool stuff.

When the market crashed hard, it was horrific for me. Within less than thirty days, I went from being worth $47 million to being worth negative $2 million. Talk about a shock to the system! Here was that familiar sinking feeling—a throwback to losing my stuff, just like when I was a little kid. Once again, I was feeling alone in the pain of having things taken from me.

I was completely wiped out. Losing my cars, that dream home, not to mention my dignity and pride, was nothing short of devastating. I was absolutely blindsided. I thank God for my network of people willing to help me through that time.

My networks were shifting once again. Each time there's a pivot on your life path, there's obviously a change in your routine and your needs. What I needed at that moment was funding. A contract. I found myself in the street fight of my life. I had to make some big choices. Not all of them were stellar. Far from it. I made the mistake of trusting a bank, and it totally screwed us over.

I had a recovery strategy in place with a contract with GGP on the table worth $1 million. More contracts were coming in. I was daring to feel a bit hopeful once again. Then virtually overnight, the bank called in my note. In violation of our contract with them, they sent letters to all my customers, telling them they now had to send all their payments directly to the bank.

Because I had such a good relationship with all my customers, I called them as soon as I caught wind of the letters. They all asked, "What do you want me to do?" I had to say, "I'm not sure just yet. Let me figure this out." In the fastest amount of time possible, I packaged up everything in the warehouse.

Unfortunately, I had to lay off a lot of people. That was the hardest part. I remember crying when I was forced to lay off my father-in-law. He said, "I'll be okay. Just take care of my daughter." I was in the process of acquiring a company going under just before the shit hit the fan. Funny enough, I wound up allowing them to acquire me! It was the craziest business deal, but it helped pull my bacon out of the fire.

I restructured and reformulated another company with that new management. We worked up several documents and stipulations that included my staying on as a shareholder. I was able to reverse the program.

We lost the big house, of course, and needed a new home. I called a doctor friend of mine and laid it on the line. "I need a house." He didn't hesitate. "Go pick one out—I'll buy it. You'll rent from me for two years, and then you'll buy it back for me for $1—plus the value of the house. I'm going to make a whopping $1 off of you." Talk about a deal you can't refuse! I'm still living in that house today.

My brother-in-law had a car dealership. I told him, "I have to turn in my two Lincolns, and need two affordable cars." Two lower-priced cars were provided to me for minimal amounts. I restructured the business, and we generated close to $2 million in the next year. We built an entire CRM company out of the dust and rubble of that stock-market crash.

I worked my way up in business through the same network that helped me when I was in deep trouble. That reinforced for me that if you just honestly let the people in your network know that you need help, that you need to create a way to take that next step, they'll show up like nobody's business.

I completely understood what George Bailey felt in the classic film *It's a Wonderful Life,* when his friends, neighbors, and family showed up in his darkest hour. That is a must-watch movie for me. I cry every single time, feeling myself in that same scene.

I share this to illustrate how building solid networking relationships can provide you with support, not only in good times but in bad ones as well. Was losing everything mortifying? Absolutely. That's what made it so difficult to share for a long time. The good news is my network and the relationships within it rose to the challenge with me and helped me not only recover, but to bounce back bigger than ever.

It took me some time to realize in retrospect that branding can include being known as a "comeback kid." Life by nature throws everyone a curve now and again. But with the support of your network and your social team, you can hang in there, rebuild, and shine brighter than before. I did it, and so can you.

Power Move: When you get hit with a big defeat, a curve, something out of your control - know you are in control of what you feel and what you do.

This is the extreme part of fear we all know. So step back, breathe, and then think of who you can connect with to talk it out. Know that you have the power within you to get up and go for your next level of greatness.

Know that you are a worthy person and go for what you were made to do. Know that you deserve the best. You are here for a reason. Keep moving!

Get Vulnerable. Get Really Vulnerable.

We help our clients humanize their brand by taking their best stories and sharing them with our networks. For example, take the story of a good friend of mine, Miri Rodriguez. She started out working in social media at Microsoft where she explored innovative ways to effectively connect with her audience through the magic of storytelling. Her storytelling acumen eventually lead to her attaining a role as "Storyteller in Core Services Engineering and Operations" at Microsoft.

In her role she has been able to unearth deep, empathetic, human stories from engineers working on extensive technical projects at Microsoft. She takes the engineers, those who write the code behind Office, Word, Excel, and other programs, and brings their human stories to the forefront. She teaches them to uncover their personal stories and how to tell them digitally and in person. She does such a beautiful job.

She's a wonderful resource with a wealth of knowledge. Miri is a caring mom who leads by example with her stories as the powerful tool that creates interest and engagement in her audience. Today, Miri has her own Storytelling course on the marketplace. She leads by example with her stories as the powerful tool that creates interest and engagement in her audience. She is a true thought leader, focused in a rapidly growing space.

Miri's success demonstrates that when an organization agrees to humanize itself through successful storytelling, the whole organization benefits. Doing so develops sustained connection and empowerment between employees, and then the ripple effect extends it out through one's customers. There's no stopping it. So many companies now have started realizing the power of tapping into the richness of the real stories of employees.

Miri got her start in the world of social media while working with the Chicago Red Stars. There she served as Marketing and New Media Manager back in 2008. Later, she took a position at Garrett Popcorn as Associate Director of Digital and Social Media.

Now at McDonald's Corporation, she oversees digital communications (web, paid search, social) as well as the corporate social media channels (Twitter, LinkedIn, Instagram, and YouTube), which is different than saying, "I oversee all of the 28,000 social media channels worldwide." Miri has also worked with over 300 athletes, executives, teams, companies, brands and nonprofits on developing their social media marketing strategies in the last ten years.

Today, wise companies are tapping into the stories of their people on the inside to share their stories on the outside. This practice can further lead to customers telling stories. The key here is to share authentically, which means allowing yourself to be vulnerable. As a result, you make deeper, more real connections.

These new relationships result in dynamic shifts and improvements within your organization, and the companies you interact with regularly. Whether you're a company of 1 or 20,000, it doesn't matter. The minute you decide to build a brand that is "real," you're going to experience a new level of success.

Power Move: *Journal*.

Write down the parts of yourself that you are afraid to tell people about, or are afraid for people to know. Write as if no one will read them. Next, pick someone you trust and share those things with them. Notice and then feel your networking partner's reaction. If you get a positive reaction, mark that as one of your impact stories, one that moves people.

This is an indicator of the part in you that creates who you are. It's that part of you that you should share. As Deepak Chopra points out, "Yes, in all my research, the greatest leaders looked inward and were able to tell a good story with authenticity and passion."

FIRST, Personal Power. Share Your Story.

As we start warming clients up in their storytelling process, we begin by having them focus on their industry. It's easy for them to talk about these things. As we get beyond asking what their goals are and who the target client or target partner is, we get a line of questioning that starts out with "What's one thing that you love about your industry?"

People will start to talk about it. This brings out their voice and even part of their story when they enthuse, "Oh, I love that the clients are receptive to what we have, and it makes it easy to sell," or whatever it is for them. That gets them into that love part.

Next, we ask, "What do you really dislike about your industry?" That launches them into a frenzy of truth telling! About midway into it, they throw up a wall. "Wait! You're not going to put this in, right?" We assure them, "No, no, no. Just keep flowing."

One thing we tell our clients is that it's the same principle that a lot of famous songwriters use. The very best songwriters "write *for* the wastebasket" -- as if no one's ever going to read it. That's when your heart and gut start to flow and your head steps aside.

When people are filling out things with us or telling us things, we say, "Just flow, then we'll pick out the best pieces and the parts that we think are most effective for you. Next, we'll work through it that way."

People start to loosen up and go on, "Okay. You know what I really hate about this industry?" It's amazing how they almost always automatically transfer the word "dislike" into "hate." They get emotional. That's when some of the juice comes out.

We'll follow that up with, "What value or values does your organization stand for?" At this point, they're talking about what values look like or mean to them. It tells us a little about their identity. Their voice starts to come through because they're starting to tell the truth. Next, we ask, "What impact does your organization's value and reputation have on you?" We get a relationship out of them—between themselves, their organization, and the industry. Again, it doesn't matter what size the organization is.

Then we get to the fun part. I always ran around as a child pretending to be a superhero. This fantasy helped me create a safe place to put on a mask and a cape and go out to "Save the world!" I still do this from time to time, but that's a whole different story.

In our trainings, we ask our audience members, "What would your superhero name be?" We have them christen themselves. A lot of times, they'll say things such as, "Well, I'm like the Superwoman of real estate," or "I'm the Spiderman of insurance because I connect all these people, and I blend all this stuff together." It's funny how we get people into that fun place. We've taken them through the light and the dark side of their industry and led them back into "What would your superhero name be?"

My favorite follow-up question is, "What is your main superpower?" By now they're really into this role playing mindset and say something like, "I can process stuff for my clients faster than anybody in the world, and that's my superpower!"

Then we get into whether they're doing things alone, or if part of their superpower is working with other people. By this point we have them answer the questions: What's your style? Are you fashionable, professional, trendy, geeky? What is your angle?

Although we can pretty accurately guess their style by their appearance, this set of questions gets them thinking differently. We get to this cool part about who they really are and what they sound like. We're capturing this, recording it, and determining how this person feels and what fits best on them.

It's like going to pick out a suit. You think it looks good on the hanger, but you have to determine how it looks once you've put it on and walked around in it. Is it comfortable? Does some part of it need to be altered to make it a perfect fit?

Next, we get into the passion question: "How did you discover your passion for what you do?" This is compelling because we hear about how they started in the beginning. It could have been thirty or forty years ago, much like working on the circuit. For me, for example, it comes down to, "Wow, I had this move from England to the south side of Chicago, to hospitality, to now." It's usually a major epiphany.

We'll get this cool juicy part about how they discovered their passion. How did they get started? I just love that part when it comes out. You see their face and body language change. A lot of times, they fall back in love with their business when they get to this point.

Almost immediately when we have them at that moment, we press onward. "So, what drives you?

NOW what gets you out of bed in the morning? What motivates you in your personal and professional life?"

We then go for the *whys*. I like this because it connects the past with the present, which obviously helps drive them to the future. This is just some of the cool juicy stuff we hear when we finally get people to that point of who they are, why they're doing this, what their story is, and taking them to that next level.

We're getting a feel and a voice for this person. We then determine what makes them different. They might be an attorney, an accountant, an insurance person, or a management consultant. We ask, "Why are you different? What sets you apart?"

That's when we start getting into individualized value proposition. Their responses run along the lines of, "Well, I'm different because I've got these superpowers." It's funny how they start tying this all together. "Nobody can touch me in this! Nobody's as good as me at this!" and "This is what makes me unique. I go above and beyond like nobody else!"

It's funny when you start weaving these questions in a certain order, it drives the emotions back and forth. A lot of them are connected, yet they're different. The next portion involves questions such as, "What do you want to become? What's your vision?"

We go from setting goals in the beginning, to "What do you want to become?" Their usual response is "Well, I want to leave a legacy, and I want to have a nonprofit. I want to do *this or that*." We keep digging for the deeper stuff by pursuing that tack. "What do you want to become in the future?"

See Yourself Being *FIRST*

I know that everybody reading this book has different beliefs, but it says in the Bible, Proverbs 29:18, "Without a vision, people will perish." From the earliest of times, having a personal vision for one's life has been important. It's about becoming all you can be by taking the journey from where you are now to where you want to be. If you can wrap the past with the present and future, you start getting a whole picture and truly find your voice.

It took eight years for us to grow to the place where our company is today. We just hit 120,000 people who have trained with us through Social Jack. Social teaming is one of the most critical pieces of the ecosystem we've created there. Our mission is to empower others and walk with them on their journey to be authentic and realize their full potential. To this end we ask everyone in our company to be a coach or trainer in some capacity. By teaching others, they learn more about the subjects they teach as well as about themselves.

The branding piece of that uniqueness is what this chapter's about. Branding's origin derived from branding cattle, but it has evolved as words and technology have advanced. Today branding is focused on the individual as much or even more so than the company.

For example, we see savvy companies experience significant growth by taking the time to work with their senior leaders and other high potentials to help them build their own brands. This strategy has then enabled companies to become more human and, as a result, more engaging to their markets.

These companies, through their top performers, are building their company brand rapidly. Both the company and their branded employees are more relatable. The focus and leverage are on the values the company holds and their employees espouse.

Ask yourself, "What are my company's values, and how do they relate to my personal values?" Your company's values should come from your people. This is about leadership. Once you become transparent and start to become authentic, you will start to lead. You show you are human which helps others better relate to you -- all of you.

In contrast, if you share a "false self" as the boss or leader, your actions could slowly build a toxic atmosphere and break down your entire organization, causing operations to grind to a halt.

Don't hang on to your false self because you fear the outcome that might result from your authenticity. Trust will breakdown and you will have an unstable culture. It's time to be genuine and then share yourself and your vision with the world and allow others around you to do the same.

Play *FIRST*. Then Work.

Once we've reached the point of getting our client's voice out to world, it's time to have fun. The question here is, "What do you love to do when you're not working?" When we ask our clients this, they start playing by responding with things such as, "Oh, I love baseball. I used to play. Every time somebody says the word 'baseball,' I see myself on the sandlot playing and then getting to the all-star game. And then I just became this whole different person because of team sports."

We'll suggest, "Just play full out here. What do you love to do?" The answer may be, "I love spending time with my family," or "I love running in a marathon because *[fill in the blank]*." This helps those going through this process connect from their heart to their head.

Next, we ask, "What's your personal brand statement? In other words, what's your *headline* to the world, and how do you want to be known?" They just go for it. We encourage them to have a lot of fun with this, to *play*. We help them play with their work—to be social, to be human.

This was the grand finale of my realization when I was doing my own work. When I felt like I should just spend my time focusing on my work, I'd think, *Oh, but all my friends are out there playing and having fun. I want to go out and play with my friends. Yet, I've got all this work to do.* A back-and-forth conflicted conversation was going on incessantly in my head. However, one day I realized,

Oh...! I know. . . we can play at work!

In fact, today in our own company, we have an *Ambassador of Fun*. I assign somebody to this role so that if I'm working too hard, they coach me to play. I tell people around me all the time, "I want to make sure that I'm playing." Just like I'm playing while I'm writing this book. I'm having fun, telling stories, and reminiscing. It's not something I *have* to do. It's something that I *want* to do because it's playful, fun, and I'm helping people.

While doing that, I'm going through all my emotions (fear, hurt, sadness, and joy), playing with those and having fun with them. It's something I can't wait to do when I wake up. That's the way every day should be for you, your job, your work, and your story. And it needs to be told.

Incorporating play into work is like putting lights on the Christmas tree. Whatever religion someone may be, when they see these beautiful lights go up, or they walk into a room and there's dazzling candlelight, that's what the play piece is. It just brings everything to that visceral, deeper, connective level. Playing while working brings out the best in us as humans. The love and the caring emerge organically. It creates that pizazz, that bright light enhancement.

Today's workforce often works 10-plus hours per day. That's another reason that it's so crucial to weave play into the workday and make it a center point. When the pendulum's so far over into the work side of things, without play, the stress factor is excessively high, and productivity tends to hit an all-time low.

Companies that get the importance of having the work space stay in balance by allowing their employees to play at times are on to something major. They find that this leverages the talents that those people have to contribute. Zappos Shoes is an outstanding example. They have effectively incorporated play into their work space. Their culture and values include a section called *Create Fun and a Little Weirdness!* (https://www.zappos.com/core-values)

Interviews with their employees consistently reflect how much they love working there.

Power Move: *Know the simple steps of "being" with yourself and others.*

Know that when you are at work you can also have fun, and play. Schedule breaks in your day to simply breathe, connect with others, and take in smiles and compliments. Let it feed you energy and use that to put forward the very best version of *you* into your workday. It will inspire those around you as well!

BUILD YOUR FIRST
Social Team

Over the last decade, I created a concept called "social teaming" by blending a number of networking methodologies that I had learned and practiced. Later, I also blended in lessons I learned as a result of my family's military history.

The two may seem separate and disconnected on the surface, but I'll point out how I have discovered some similarities and overlap between those areas. First, though, I'll share some stories about folks who have built successful social teams. Then I'll come back to share the steps of how you can do the same.

Take, for example, my client and good friend Brian, the owner of a real estate company. Like many folks in that business, he has experienced incredibly successful times, but also tough downturns. When I met Brian he had recently suffered some significant losses in his business and felt extremely alone. But after going through our Social Jack training, he learned how to create successful results by reinventing himself and his network through social teaming.

When I introduced the idea of scouting and drafting a social team, we called the process, "Two Old, Two New." This meant you were to first play two of your old players from your current team sheet, and then you would play with two new players. I'll be sharing more about this process as you continue reading, and I will give you the Power Moves to make it so in your own experience.

After going through our program, Brian went on to build a powerful new real estate company in Silicon Valley. He is an outstanding example of what one can achieve by applying a solid social media methodology. He truly reinvented himself and his brand, which also involved creating an entirely new team. Now he teaches our techniques in every one of his real estate courses. Brian sends all his team through our training. He knows the power of learning to build the best social team possible.

This process is not just about revamping yourself. It's also about learning how to make life-altering shifts. This holds true whether you change industries, product lines, or countries. It doesn't matter. You can change your team or scout and draft a new team anytime. Or you can take your current team and use that to draft a new one.

Kids Programs and Self-Reflection. On the Street

This aspect of my journey began about ten years ago when I was doing some research on the internet about kids and generational differences in mental health struggles. At the time, my son, Jackson was ten, and learning way too much on the school bus. Meanwhile, my daughter, Sydney, age six, was right behind him. I wanted to prepare as a parent to deal with the world of the internet and especially social media, which was fairly new at the time. My search resulted in discovering horrific stories of pre-teen and teen suicides with staggeringly high statistics.

One story, for example, involved a young girl who was made fun of and bullied online by her peers, who said she was ugly and that no one liked her. The perpetrator was thought to be a friend at school, but it turned out that it was that friend's mom, who was jealous of the girl.

This young innocent girl, only eleven at the time, was one day found in her closet. She had hanged herself. I remember being pretty shook up for about a week after reading that story. I knew I had to do something to help other children who might be experiencing the same type of pain. Imagine how much fear this gave me as a parent.

Because I personally lost friends to suicide when I was a teenager, this jumped out at me in a big way. Remember early in the book when I shared with you that I was in a gang, or more of rat pack back then? Well, once while at a beach bonfire with a bunch of my buddies, another gang descended on our party. I watched in horror as one of them shot and killed a friend of mine. I stayed back, doing my best to protect my friends up in the dunes. I'll never forget that awful night.

I saw more than my share of tragedy during high school, which fueled my deep yearning to get out of that place. Again, it was this feeling of wherever I am, it's not safe. I need to get somewhere else. A couple of my high school friends committed suicide. That's another life event you never can shake.

Although today's world is different in many ways, one common thread that still runs through it is the constant tragedies that occur daily. One series of tragedies that I am most sensitive to are the number of kids who feel so alone and hopeless that they eventually convince themselves that ending their lives is their only alternative. The big difference today from when I was a teen is that often, right up until their final hours, they reach out on social media. There are cases of many who tried to get some sense of belonging or assurance from doing this, but sadly, nothing came in time.

As a result, I've seen a preponderance of students who tweet out, "I can't take it anymore, it's over." They then end their young lives. It makes me weep every time. Having been an at-risk, lonely kid myself and knowing several friends who took their own lives, I knew I had to do *something*.

These younger people were trapping their secret self, deep inside. It became so painful that they felt they couldn't let the world know who they really were or that if they tried to, nobody cared. This was such a parallel to the pain I personally experienced in my youth that there was no way I was going to sit idly by when I knew I had something to offer.

We now offer social team building at all levels of education—grade school through graduate school. In the past decade, we've done more than twenty youth programs at churches, as well as universities and both private and public schools. We don't just train the students. We include their families and teachers in the training. At times, we've packed the auditoriums with those in attendance. I estimate we've reached well over 2,000 people in that program, both young and old.

We include the adults in the kids' lives because if we were simply teaching the young people, there wouldn't be a sustainability factor that carried on. Often the parents are the ones who need to understand the most what we have to share. They're the ones who believe their children should live in the "box" or paradigm in which they raised them.

One of the biggest challenges we face with this is that today's world is a unique place to grow up. Kids are different from their parents, who are different from their kids' grandparents. Technology has contributed in a huge way to all of this. Parents today need to find ways to develop relationships with their children, and then maintain those relationships.

Our current five-year plan is to create a nonprofit, and then leverage the power of our corporate sponsorships to go into the schools and educational systems that can't afford to have our program. Our goal is to deputize these students. We want to empower them to become leaders in digital citizenship, helping those younger than them learn to be better.

We want adults teaching the graduate program. We also want graduate students or graduates teaching the undergrads. In turn, we want the undergrads teaching high school, high school students teaching middle school, and middle school teaching grade school.

By providing them with ongoing social connection knowledge, they build skill sets that will create better networks that will last their lifetime. As a result, these kids can become leaders of a strong social support to future generations coming up behind them. Another win-win is that as these kids teach one another, they further build their skills.

A major goal of ours is to create a better social environment at the foundation. By taking our expertise in the business world and combining that with social skills training, we're providing them with tools they can use for the rest of their lives. As my friend Melissa G. Wilson, author and networking expert, points out, we're coming up through the various levels of schooling, building a beautiful, socially strong bridge and pathway for these kids to have incredible lives versus risky ones.

When we began teaching social team building nearly a decade ago in grad schools and universities, we learned a lot from the interactivity that occurred. We found it vital to include the fact that students didn't have to wait for their degree to build their social team. We tell them, "Do it right now." In fact, in grad school, we teach them that you can make *Power Moves*. Your professors, other students, working at internships—these people are all part of your current team.

As a result, within eight weeks, we've seen record-breaking successes in the grad school program. These are motivated young adults holding down full-time jobs while finishing their degrees. We learned that when they built their social teams and created shifts, they were getting promoted and hired into new and better positions within just eight weeks! I saw this as a true blessing.

One young lady, for example, worked the desk at our local gym. I would always see her studying medical books. I asked her why she was not currently working in the healthcare area. She said she was waiting for her degree. I asked, "Why?" She said that is what she was told. I asked, "Are you on LinkedIn?" She said that she was, but her profile did not currently represent her well. I gave her some easy assignments to spruce up her profile, but the real magic came when we built her social team from the people she already knew!

We helped her connect to professors, friends, family members in nursing, etc. She was amazed at how she quickly found over 50 connections with whom she had relationships in the medical field. A few weeks passed before I saw her again. I asked her how everything was going in her world. She looked at me with glistening eyes and exclaimed with a huge smile, "I'm leaving for a medical internship. Thank you sooo much for all your help!" I was so appreciative that I was able to make a difference in her life.

This experience demonstrated to me that despite all the challenges, this world is filled with potential and hope. There are many scenarios where we could see countless numbers of kids emerging as superstars. Instead, we're breeding a culture of loneliness and rejection, and far too often they decide to kill themselves. Many times, the adults around them don't recognize the power that these kids have. They don't see what's right in front of them.

This is a driving force behind why my team and I are putting our programs out there as a wake-up call. It will alert adults that we're in grave danger of losing our children because people are not getting social connection right. It's morphing into something so gray that it's the opposite of the connection it was intended to foster.

By relearning how to navigate today's online social experience, we believe that a powerful sense of connection can rise to its full potential. If we can play even a small part in bringing this to pass, it's worth whatever effort(s) it takes.

The connection here is quite parallel to how alone an entrepreneur or business leader can feel at times. In other words, when their business faces challenges and they're tempted to just retreat or take it all on as a one-man or one-woman show, those feelings of aloneness and being overwhelmed are quite similar to the emotions a teen goes through while being bullied and/or struggling with low self-esteem.

At that point, the business becomes too painful. They lose the love of their business. As a result, it becomes toxic and/or fails. I want to encourage business leaders and thought leaders to always ask for help from their networks before allowing that to happen.

From Softball to Theater: A Case of Bullying

I shared earlier that my background in baseball started when my dad remarried, and we moved to a neighborhood where sandlot ball was incredibly popular. After working on getting to know some of the kids there, I was invited to play. However, I was also the last to be picked. But I decided to work hard on improving my abilities in the game.

It was my dad, though, who helped me graduate from a mediocre player to a baseball all-star. To this end, he would come home from work every single day and spend hours hitting balls to me, and we'd practice and practice and practice some more.

Meanwhile, as I was improving my game skills, I was also networking and befriending more of the kids, especially the baseball team captains. As I got better at the game and more well-known, I found myself one day being picked first rather than last. That was a major motivator for me. I remember I was even selected as captain at one point, so I got to pick my own team.

Then it got scarier. I now was ready for Little League. This meant over 200 other kids also trying out. I didn't know most of them as they were from other neighborhoods. Suddenly, again, I was unsure of myself. I started making a lot of mistakes. However, I was able to get on a team and, once again, started practicing between games. Eventually, I reached the point where I had one of the top batting averages, top home runs, multiple bases, and more.

With Little League, my stepmom started helping me. Sometimes she would award me a quarter for every base I made. Translation: I made $1.50 for every home run I hit. She would track the bases I made on a 5x7 index card, and review with them me after every game. I learned the value of hard work paying off at a very young age! My stepmom was all about hard work and tracking stuff, so, with the help of my first *social team*, which was my mom, dad, and the sandlot guys, I became a great baseball player during that time.

I've witnessed the parallel as my daughter Sydney's path in softball became the same as mine. I find this so interesting. When she was around nine years old, someone watching her play saw that she had some raw talent. By the age of ten, she was drafted by the White Sox Travel Ball Team. At that point, she was a talented player who still needed some work. So we worked with her and got her some lessons.I would play with her at times. She worked super hard at getting better and better.

She usually played some of the toughest positions on the field, like catcher and third base. She would often come home pretty banged up and bruised, and we had to take her on a few trips to the ER, but she hung in there. Sometimes she'd come home with cleat marks on her ankles, so you can't tell me that girls aren't as tough as boys when it comes to sports!

Off the field, she always had tremendous hand-eye coordination when playing video games. She was nothing short of phenomenal at that. Many times, she would be the one who would finish the rounds of games that her older brother had started. I'm convinced that coordination crossed over into her hitting skills.

As she got older, she began going to tryouts for higher level teams. We didn't have connections in those circles as much as we did in our hometown's softball world. So sometimes she'd get nervous at tryouts and would make a few flubs, and not get selected.

She got turned down by several teams, but she kept at it. Finally, one team gave her a chance and drafted her. It was going to be one of her last tryouts for the summer because a couple of the best teams in town hadn't taken her. But once she joined this team, she made many friends and connections. It was amazing.

She became a top player, somebody that they could count on. This was so fantastic for her self-esteem. Before this, she had been getting benched a lot for things like dropping balls in the outfield, and just being made to feel that she was not such a hot player. It was toxic to get benched and not coached, tough on the self-esteem.

Now, because this team gave her a shot, she realized all that self-defeatism was in her head. Now she started playing catcher and third base. She tried out for a few other positions because the team required that you play at least two.

As her confidence grew, it was amazing to watch her get up to bat. Before, most of the time she wouldn't hit the ball far enough to get on base. It was a cool time for Sydney and her proud family, too. The telling difference was that these girls were her solid team.

Because of her newfound confidence, her social network grew and improved dramatically. She also built her reputation as a stellar player, and her powerful team helped her draft into better teams in the future. Her focused efforts helped Sydney build to the point where she was a walk-on. She was on a state championship team, playing up in age and with girls older than her.

Sydney was considered a *lockdown walk-on*. We learned that, surprisingly, the team's attitude was that she didn't have to try out to see if they wanted her. They already wanted her and only hoped she wanted them! This blew me away. As she played in many tournaments, we were on the road with her continuously.

But then after about five years, to our surprise, during mid-season break while on our way to a tournament, she told us she wasn't happy playing softball anymore. I have always told Sydney that life's too short to stay in a job you hate. So I supported her decision when she came to me and said, "I'm just not happy playing. It doesn't feel right anymore. Dad, you told me if I don't love it, that I need to make a change. I'm ready to do that now."

When Sydney broke the news to her coach, he was stunned. Here was a star player with a .628 batting average, and she was quitting. It was crazy! We watched as she handed over her $250 Louisville Slugger bat to the coach's daughter. Next, she gave her catcher's gear to another girl, and then she hung up her cleats, once and for all. We knew she was dead serious. This was real, and it was necessary for her to make a shift.

This happened right before her freshman year of high school. A scout was working on her behalf to garner college scholarships. On one hand, it was heartbreaking for us to see her walk away from that opportunity, but we also knew that this was the right move for her.

An interesting side effect that occurred was that now her network, her social team, needed to change. She needed to shift from the network she formed from being on a ball field to going back to her first love: performing onstage. She wasn't just changing teams, she was changing careers. She has an amazing voice, and now she had a renewed burning desire to get back on stage and into musicals.

All of a sudden, she started getting into auditions and plays. In some ways, my son Jackson had paved the way for her. When he was in high school, he became involved in theater. The theater network was his *homies*, his social network. So he tapped into his social team, and we tapped into ours that had grown because of years of supporting our local community theater.

We used our respective networks to help Sydney build her network. As a result, she was already *known* before she started school there. Therefore, she seamlessly made the transition from the softball field to the theatrical stage.

Then because of her incredible voice and support network, Sydney had a built-in fan base. She could never try out for any theater during the softball years because she was always in tournaments. But now, the directors and theater groups were awestruck, often saying things like, "Oh, my gosh, is Sydney really available?"

Now, instead of having softball parties, we had theater friends, some who were theater parents themselves. It was so wonderful to see her making the transformation, and being genuinely happy because of it. Within her first year of high school, she beat out a whole lot of girls by getting the lead role in the spring musical. She was a freshman, so she got cast instead of any of the upper class girls.

Today, Sydney tends to favor Instagram and some other social media outlets over Twitter, but some of those older theater girls started bashing her indirectly by posting things like, "It's not fair—a freshman shouldn't get a role when there's a senior that has worked hard to deserve it." That progressed into more in-depth social media bashing and bullying.

Others in her new network immediately came to her defense and told them to stop. Because of their supportive outreach, the bullying came to a grinding halt. A lot of people supported her in that role, and she did an amazing job. She's been getting leads and significant roles ever since, and at the writing of this book, she's only a sophomore.

This chapter is also about finding your voice to make requests. I have always done my best to teach my kids and clients, and, especially women, to speak up for themselves. Take the book, *Women Don't Ask*, written by two female Yale professors. The results of their studies show that all too often women don't make powerful requests of others. I believe that's one incredible gift that social teaming offers. A huge factor in building a team is about finding your voice and making requests. This is all about what we call, "The Ask."

The most important thing to remember here is that you have to continuously build your social team. Don't wait for others to reach out to you. This social world is so ripe with opportunities. When you don't ask, you lose out on opportunities. Therefore, you must make building your team a priority for yourself as well as for those in your organization.

Social Influence: Sports and the Military

As I shared in the introduction, I grew up playing team sports, including baseball, football, and wrestling. Wrestling is unique from the rest in that you compete as an individual, though you win or lose as a team because your points contribute to team points.

Growing up in Chicago, there were incredibly long streaks of bad professional sports teams' performance. Along the way, we had a few tastes of excellent championship teams, but as most Chicago sports fans know, we're well acquainted with heartbreak.

I was always a Chicago Bears fan. I remember watching them with my dad during the '70s with fond memories of him screaming regularly at the TV. My mom even got him a sponge to throw at the TV when he was especially frustrated with their plays.

Every sports fan, Chicagoan or not, can relate at one time or another to this picture. When we see a team's talent and potential, it's maddening to figure out why they can't win. When the '85 Bears won the Super Bowl, for example, I thought, "Wow! What's the difference between this team and all the previous ones that had such lousy losing streaks?"

As for baseball in Chicago, you're either a Cubs or a Sox fan. My mom was a big Sox fan. Sometimes we'd go to the games. It was fun. Sometimes they had a good team, but many times they didn't.

As an adult, I became a Cubs fan and bought season tickets. They'd win the division, and it would be exciting. Then we'd get our hopes up and think, "This is the year!" But it took 108 years of hoping they would win the World Series. In 2016, they finally did.

I also held Bulls' tickets when Michael Jordan was on the roster. By then, I was studying what made the makeup of that team different than previous ones. My friends would tell me, "Oh, yeah, I can remember getting in to see Michael Jordan when he was first a Bulls player. Tickets were only $20. We could even high five him coming out of the tunnel. Now you can't touch a ticket near the tunnel for under $200 a game, and they are not that good!" The question in my mind once again was, "Okay, what's the difference here?" Same with the Blackhawks in hockey.

I started studying successful championship teams. I had the pleasure of being connected to some folks in the Chicago Bears' office, including some of the scouts. Because of my curiosity, which had grown stronger over the years, I asked, "What do you guys do? How do you determine the best players on the team?"

The responses I got were, "Well, it's not just the individual, but it's how that person fits within the culture of the team and whether he or she has a similar mission and set of values. Some players are very good extreme sports players; others play for themselves. Their goal is to go from, say, $2 million a year to $20 million a year, and they'll do whatever it takes. And sometimes they don't hold the team in high regard."

I probed a bit more, asking, "What are the different qualities that you look for?" They came back with, "We meet with the general manager and team owners. Then we identify who would be good in terms of makeup for the team; what components or jobs within the team are missing, and who can help get us to a championship."

The more I heard these types of comments, it became apparent it was a repeating pattern. It wasn't always about talent. Sometimes it was about connection *among* the players and being a good *fit.*

That led to my next question, "How do you find these players?" Their reply was, "Quite honestly, it's nonstop networking. It's about finding those scouts out there who are good at discovering these future top players. Then we connect to them through their parents or whomever necessary so that we reach these potential superstars before anyone else does."

Finally, one other burning question came to the forefront, "So when is scouting season for you guys? Is it the months before Draft Day, or just when does it happen?" Their answer? "It's every day. We're constantly looking, and always building relationships. Sometimes we spend holidays with the families of potential players. It's all about relationships and your network."

The more I learned about this, the more I was amazed to find parallels between sports and business. I learn that top performers in the business world had robust networks with incredible connections. They also had tremendous dedication to building their careers. That led to ensuring that they created a championship "team" in their industry. They were, or had, the ultimate scouts. Thus, the sports puzzle pieces coming into focus began laying the foundation for social team building.

On the military side, many of my family members were in the service, including my dad. I grew up being intrigued by this way of life. The military aspect of my social teaming stems from a U.S. Army-developed science called *network science*. Here, multiple scientists participated and discovered there was a natural and unnatural order to the way networks are organized. Of course, they use the knowledge they discovered for military purposes. So, for example, the U.S. implemented network science to determine when to go after Saddam Hussein and Osama bin Laden.

There, they used network science to figure out which cells or clusters of people had formed who were connected to Saddam Hussein and Osama bin Laden - their targets. To break it down further, there are four components to this. One is *nodes,* which represent an individual in any network. You and I, in this case, would be individual nodes.

Further, when two people connect, you have two *targeted* nodes. Note that LinkedIn has built their framework on a three-degree network model which means that you are able to connect through those in your network (your first-degree connections) to those your first degree know (your second- degree connections) and then to those they know (your third-degree connections). When you think of "targeted nodes" with social team building, it's crucial to remember the word, "target."

The third component of network science consists of *clusters*. A cluster is made up of several linked nodes of like-minded people. In the business world, this might look like you seeking to connect through your network to find an executive vice president in manufacturing. When you connect to him or her that becomes a *link*. They start to form several linked nodes, which then blossom into a *cluster*. You then have a cluster of manufacturing V.P.s and other top people related to them.

Finally, the fourth component is a *hub,* which is a large cluster. Again, thinking of those people you wish to target to become part of your network, these could be, for example, leaders within a Fortune 500 company such as GE, Microsoft, or Google. These companies are big hubs. Within them here are other hubs or networks representing company divisions, departments, industries, etc.

This is how I'd like you to think when it comes to forming and building your networks, a.k.a. social teams. Network science provides a template that you can tap into to connect to your ideal targets. (Note the crossover and overlap between sports and military science.)

As I started looking at the science of networks by studying successful companies, I included in my research corporate and sales executives who had elevated themselves quickly to one level of success after another.

One common factor they shared was their ability to build powerful networks. They had people in their networks with whom they had built extreme levels of trust and connection. Whatever their next destination might be, they were generating high levels of referrals—not just from one, two or three people but from ten or up to twenty people.

This is how sports teams work, as they are consistently scouting and drafting all the time to bring top-performing players into their teams.

My passion for social networking research is how I developed *social teaming* as a way to help others scout, draft, and score their ideal teams (networks). Many times in our Social Jack classes, we'll say, "Describe your championship. What are you looking to achieve? Are you going for the Super Bowl of business? Are you reaching for the World Series of your industry?" It's fun to play with those targets, or "destinations," as we call them.

The simplicity of the system is a big part of its beauty. Breaking this down into five sections, in the first section, place the top five people in your network. Here your focus is on building extended relationships with them and their network (your second degree). You're all on the same path with the goal of winning and becoming champions in your industry or business. Your networks are well aligned, and there's a mutuality and reciprocity, as well as respect, building between you.

These could be your ideal starting players, so you're looking for five starters. When we do this in a class, it's interesting how long it takes people to just get their first player named. In fact, you're probably wondering right now, "Hmm, what does that look like?" In the next section of this chapter, I'll take you through the steps to help you make sense of it all.

Next, it's time to determine your 10 *bench players.* These are outstanding players who can jump in if your starters need to take a break for some reason. They can just step up and fill that role, helping each of your respective teams win "championships." They're valuable players even though they are your bench.

Next you create a field of 25 who comprise your *practice/recruiting squad.* They are the rest of your team from which you pull to help carry you the rest of the way. With all of these players in your social team network, you're constantly building relationships.

People on my social team—whether they've been on there for a short while or for many years—often call me up and ask, "Hey, how's our team doing? You think we'll get to the championship?" It's an exciting experience. And it's an addictive experience once you and your team start reaping the rewards.

As you see your team starting to form, please bear in mind that some people whose social teams don't win championships or hit their goals tend to get comfortable with their current team and stop scouting. They stop measuring their success and settle with the status quo. You'll notice a parallel of this in professional sports. Some cities have been through decades of losing teams. They are caught up in mediocrity.

Anyone can easily fall into that trap within their network. You want to make sure that your social-teaming activity involves scouting, drafting, scoring, and winning every day. That's why we devised the metric of 20-minutes a day of scouting and drafting so that it becomes an easy part of your daily routine, but doesn't drag out.

Within Social Jack we offer scouting and drafting as a service. However, we also keep our clients engaged and participating in the process. Learn to stay aware of when you meet somebody new. Look at them and consider whether they are a potential starter for you. Make this part of your daily life.

For example, you could bump into somebody—at Starbucks, at the airport, in a meeting, or on social media. Ask yourself, *what's their potential for building strong networking exchanges?* Is this somebody well aligned with similar values, beliefs, and goals? By consistently scouting you will build a powerful team for yourself and others.

Your *FIRST* Realization of Social Reach and Impact

Write down what you see as your goal. Once you have established what you want to achieve you can build from there. For example, say you are in business-to-business sales and your goal this year is to double your sales. Your ideal targets to achieve that goal include the CEOs, CFOs, and COOs in your database.

Your best approach would be to build a network of strong partners who can connect you to your ideal targets, and, in turn, with whom you can reciprocate. This will create even more opportunities for you all.

As you start looking at ideal targeted partnerships, you'll have an epiphany such as, "Oh, those who sell complementary products or services to the ones I'm currently selling could be good teammates." These are people in different industries who also serve your targets.

You can also go from the outside in. Here, you might connect with people currently in your network who have potential complementary partners in their network. These people would be considered your *second degree* connections. In other words, again, they are one person away from you.

The power of your existing network to provide you with a *warm introduction* or referral into those C-suite connections you want to reach is very real. As you become more skilled and experienced at making requests to connect to others, you'll manifest many more new opportunities because of your network than you initially thought.

Before the Social Media Boom

Back in the early 2000s, prior to LinkedIn or social media of any type, I was looking to work with Baxter Labs in Chicago. I used CRM (customer relations management) to map out a plan to network in there. It took quite a long time. I would ask those in my network, "Hey, is there anybody you're connected to who knows somebody at Baxter Labs?"

Though this was a primitive, slow, old-fashioned process compared to today, it still worked. I found people who were well connected, and I realized that I needed them on my team. Pretty soon, it dawned on me that I had a super powerful network. When I started finding myself sitting in many boardrooms, it felt humbling.

Remember, this whole networking world was something I was first exposed to as a busboy in a restaurant, back in my hospitality days. Even then, I could see that it was all about who you know. I had realized early on that I had all the potential within me. I figured out that if I didn't have a network, there were ways to go about building one. That's the beauty of networking. It's a forever life skill situation.

As you begin to inventory the people you already have, take time to pinpoint those with whom you communicate most. The funny thing is, if you look at whom you email and call on a regular basis, you'll begin to pick up some team players. I also want you to watch out, because some of those players aren't truly skillful; they're just people with whom you're comfortable.

Be willing to stretch as you build this initial list. Right off the bat, don't think about starters and bench players. Think of whom you call and connect with most.

You'll assign them a position later. At the get-go, you're just looking for people who match that profile and are potentially good teammates.

As you start to list those out, you can work in CRM, look on social media, access your email database, or research the contacts on your cell phone. It will dawn on you, "Well, if I'm doing this social team building officially, my players should be the people helping me thrive and drive that championship in my business world."

When I'm teaching this in a class, it's inevitable that many students get this look on their faces as it hits them that they need to work on this. A lot of them exclaim, "My current team sucks!" But that's no detriment to the people they're communicating with. It's simply that you're now conscious of playing on a team at a higher level.

It's an eye-opening discovery to recognize that those ideal players are well within your reach. Even right now, as you're reading, you begin to realize the power. Next, choose someone as a sample and go to LinkedIn. One of the great things about their site is that they're showing you the degrees of separation from your targets. You'll notice a Number 1, Number 2, or Number 3 designating how many degrees away they are from you. A Number 3 is somebody who's connected to those second-degree connections.

THE POWER OF **YOUR CONNECTIONS**

- That know YOU?
- That trust YOU?
- That have done business with YOU?
- That would recommend YOU?

NO MORE ONE TO ONE SELLING!

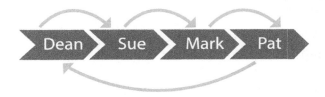

The diagram on the left shows where you start with your network while the one on the right shows the vastness of your network once you start building your team.

SOCIAL TEAMING - **3 DEGREES**

Your network has always been like this. It's just that prior to today's technology, you've never had the visibility to see a depth chart to help you understand the full power of your social team. Even if you don't have a powerful team at this moment, you can leverage the relationships that you do have to build the new relationships and team that you want. That's what the sports scouts do. They not only see the *depth* of their social team, but they also leverage it to build a *championship team*.

Start to realize your social reach. To do this, take a few moments to do a simple search on LinkedIn by typing in the title of your ideal target client or customer. For example, "CEO." Click on PEOPLE in the navigation bar at the top of your LinkedIn page. You may well be overwhelmed as you realize, "Wow! This says I have 12.5 million CEOs." But start by breaking down your connections by first-level connections and then second level, and then third-level.

Note that LinkedIn is a three-degree model. You can further refine your search by industry, geography, and a variety of other useful filters. By conducting these targeted searches, you will discover just how much ability you have to locate key targets.

As of the writing of this book, we use the power of 8,000:1. This ratio is based on some of the early calculations of one's network at three degrees. For example, if you have 300 ideal targeted contacts within your network, you are connected to 6.2 million people, on average, depending on the power of those connections and how many connections they have.

Essentially, you are connected to approximately 6.2 million professionals. This means that for every person you meet with the intent to have a relationship and make a connection on LinkedIn, you're automatically additionally connected to 8,000 new potential connections—within two degrees of you. That's huge. That's extreme power.

Power Move: *List your potential team players.*

Make a list of all the potential people you see on your team. Look them up on LinkedIn and realize the social reach and power that you have with every one of those connections.

Select Your *FIRST* Player

As you're looking for your first player (your number one draft pick), a lot of realizations and humbling feelings may come up. You may feel blessed to have that person on your team. Or you might wind up feeling ashamed, saying, "I can't believe I've been spending all the time with this weak network." It's never good to feel shame, so shake that off. The trick is to stay in a state of appreciation that you now have the skills to make this whatever you want. Remember, you've always had the ideal network within your reach. You just couldn't see it.

Recently, I suggested to a long-term client, "Because we have known one another for a long time, how about testing how much we know about each other?" We started by seeing if we knew the names of our respective children. I realized quickly that I didn't remember his daughters' names. He told me what they were. I apologized and said, "That probably hurt. We've talked about our children for ten years, and I didn't remember their names."

We had this deeply truthful conversation. It allowed me to get real with him, so that I could say, "Listen, I really want to know more about you. I care about you and the success of your business. But I also care about you personally." Recognize that you must build a level of trust and commitment to develop that high-level relationship. I give him referrals. He gives me referrals. There's no doubt there's mutuality and reciprocity. We're constantly helping each other along the way. Somebody like my client would be an ideal first player.

Power Move: *Identify your FIRST player from your list.*

Look through the list that you made. Find that *first* player who genuinely resonates with you. You might have to circle the Top 10. Pick the best one. You can start numbering the rest. Think about that, make that list, and see how that works for you.

FIRST Steps in Scouting

Remember, scouting is partially about raising your awareness, and then systematizing it. You've now found your first player, but you're faced with this collection of other potential players and, at the same time, discovering whether you want to put them on your team. This is the easiest step of new scouting techniques.

Start looking at potential players. Assess who will make the cut and become part of your team. This doesn't mean you can't you can't maintain friendships or connections with those who remain. It is simply essential that you focus on identifying the best players that will network with you at that next higher level (leveling up, as I put it).

Now choose the next player you want on your social team, and place him or her right underneath your first player on your chart. As you begin to look for other good networking partners, you will also start becoming more aware of other potential partners.

You may experience some difficulty at first. But don't overcomplicate your search. Just make sure you're getting those better players to the top of the list—your Top 5. You can put others on the bench or on the list as your *practice squad.* Once you begin to assemble your top players, you'll get into a methodology of playing them and vetting them out. But for now, scout off that initial list.

The next level of scouting involves spending time on social media or attending networking events or meetings where you can get introduced to new potential players.

Now it's time to create conversational exchanges to explore commonalities with potential partners. Here you may discover you have similar values and visions.

From this discovery, you can continue to exchange insights, connections, and opportunities.

What's beautiful about social media is that it makes everything much easier. Remember my story about needing to have at least a dozen in-person meetings with those in my network back in the early 2000s? That took place so I could better understand which connections were truly going to be the best ones when it came to becoming mutually powerful and beneficial teammates. That vetting took so much time and a lot of extra efforts. But today's technology has cut that time investment down significantly. Just make sure you are constantly scouting for the best partnerships for optimal social networking.

That being said, also appreciate the fact that if you scout daily, you will forever have a championship team in the making. Chicago is known as the "City of the Broad Shoulders." It's a nickname that comes from the fifth line of Carl Sandburg's poem, *Chicago*. Sandburg, like millions of others, saw Chicago as the city of the working class.

The Chicago of 1900 was a tough, blue-collar town. It was "stormy, husky, and brawling," a transportation hub for the nation. Unlike New York City, a financial hub, Chicago was a rough and tumble collection of agricultural, manufacturing, and financial centers. It was growing so fast its population doubled every twenty years.

Sandberg wasn't criticizing the rough image he described. He was celebrating it. He wanted his readers to see Chicago as a "man's man," one who could take on any challenge, bear it, and succeed despite overwhelming odds against it. While "the Windy City," and other nicknames describe its aspects, "City of the Broad Shoulders" illustrates the city's personality, strengths, and character. It's the foundation for the classic Chicago saying: "We're always rebuilding." It's a feeling and culture of, "We're tough. We've got this."

I'm sure this is true in many other cities as well. It's the same with social teaming. If you're strong and focused on succeeding, you're always rebuilding. This is an ongoing conscious effort. You should be scouting and drafting every day.

Power Move: *Add Scouting and Drafting to your Calendar.*

Add a consciousness activity to your calendar, and title it Scouting and Drafting. Reserve and commit 20-minutes a day for this task. Enjoy the fun of scouting potential players who may become good friends as well as members of your social team.

Select Your *FIRST Draft Picks*

Setting primary objectives during your scouting and drafting is the perfect place to start. We've already gone over goal setting and measurements. If you're in sales, you may need to book a certain number of appointments per week. You may be looking to become a better speaker and therefore get paid more for that.

Whatever your objectives, the key thing to bear in mind is that you're building a team so that your thought leadership is better known in the world. That way, people can be attracted to you through others.

As you collect new team members during your scouting and drafting process, make sure you're not just tracking them, but also taking the time to have some meetings and really get to know them. Bottom line: It's always about relationships. That's another reason why social media is so powerful.

When you find somebody you want on your team, you can look on their social media profile to get to know them better. See what they like, if they have a family, what their hobbies and interests are. They may like the same sports or cultural events that you do, or they went to the same school as you. You can tell a lot about people by doing this type of easy research. Think about this fact when you're scouting. It's powerful.

Now that you've scouted and people are rising to the top, your first draft picks are the ones you're selecting and putting on your team. Draft Day in sports typically means you have scouted all the draft picks and are now selecting. With your team sheet in front of you, you begin assembling your Top 5 starters. The good news is, unlike sports teams, you don't have to worry about a salary cap. Your only concern is a relationship score. I'll get to that in a minute.

As you select these first draft picks, don't get hung up on accomplishing all your goals at once. It's okay to not have the end-game team in sight at the moment. You'll be doing this on an ongoing basis. Enjoy the selection process and putting them into your team formation.

Go through the current list of folks you have right now. Due to the constant nature of team building, you might even have met somebody new while reading this chapter. You're going to look at your entire world through a different lens from here on out. Start selecting a slot on your team for each pick.

Starters, Bench Players, Practice Squad, and Farm Team

As you see people, you'll think, "Okay, I'll put them at bench player, or this person goes on my practice squad. I don't quite know their full potential yet, but I know I want them there."

The first 5 are your key players, your Starters. The next 10 are the Bench. Those are also critical because they support your starters. The next 25 are Practice Squad players. Everybody else for the time being goes into a bucket called the Farm Team. Most sports have a farm team from which they'll take certain draft picks, but they're uncertain of their potential just yet. So, they put them on the farm team. Your Farm Team are people you still want in your network, but are not necessarily sure at this point where or whether they belong on the team.

If you break this down into five sections, first you have your top five people in your network. Here, you're focused on building top relationships where all of you are dedicated to winning, to becoming champions in your respective industries and/or businesses. Your networks are well aligned, and you share a mutuality and reciprocity, as well as respect between you.

These could be your ideal starting players, so you're looking for five Starters. When we do this in a class, it's interesting how long it takes people to just name their first player. In fact, you're probably wondering right now, "Hmm, what does that look like?" In the next section of this chapter, I'll take you through some steps to help it all make sense.

Next, it's time to determine your 10 Bench Players. These are amazing players in their own right, who can jump in if your starters need a break for some reason. They can just step up and fill that role, helping your team win the "championship." They're very valuable players, your Bench.

Then you should also have a field of 25 who comprise your Practice/Recruiting Squad. They are the rest of your team from which you pull to help carry you the rest of the way. You're constantly building relationships in there, which will be detailed more below.

Relationship Scoring: Five Levels

As you begin assigning a level number to your relationship with each of your players, it may be a bit daunting at first. You'll be scoring these from a very one-sided position, but it's important to come up with an initial score just to test yourself. I've included a chart that shows Levels 1 through 5 in Relationship Scoring.

MY IDEAL 40 – ID40 – SOCIAL JACK SCORING VERSION - EXAMPLE

Top 5 (50 Points)		Next Top 10 (25 Points)	Next Top 25 (10 Points)	
3	Steve Cappa = 50 * 3 = 150	Lenny Potts	Betsy Williams	
3	John Smith = 50 * 3 = 150	Ken Turvill	Karen Rubens	
5	Holly Crane = 50 *5 = 250	Jim Stevens	John Franks	
1	Sally Johns = 50 * 1 = 50	Karen Bell	Kim Parks	
2	Max Burgess = 50 * 2 = 100	Desiree Kent	Joe Zuhn	
		John Warrent	RAPPORT, MUTUALITY AND RELATIONSHIP FREQUENCY FACTOR: USE THE MULTIPLIER BASED ON LEVEL OF RELATIONSHIP AND RAPPORT.	
		Liam Trent		
		Pete Miller		
	SAMPLE CALCULATION	Jan Olsher	*0 – NEVER – LITTLE OR NO TOUCH - NOT SURE WHERE WE ARE AT (WIPES OUT VALUE)	
		Lillian Martins		
			*1 = BARELY CONNECT – NO MUTUALITY - LOW TOUCH – THEY KNOW ME BUT NOT SURE OF TRUST LEVEL	
			*2 = COUPLE TIMES A YEAR – THEY KNOW ME AND TRUST ME – LOW MUTUALITY – LOW TOUCH - REFERS ME ONCE IN A WHILE	
			*3 = SEVERAL TIMES A YEAR – BETTER CONNECTION - SOME MUTUALITY - MODERATE TOUCH AND HIGHER RELIABILITY FACTOR	
			*4 = MONTHLY REFERRALS –SOME MUTUALITY - HIGER TOUCH - TRUST AND REFERS ME OFTEN	
			*5 = WOULD DO ANYTHING FOR ME – VERY MUTUAL – HIGH TOUCH - REFERS ME ALL THE TIME!)	
TOTAL OF TOP 5 = 700		TOTAL OF NEXT TOP 10 =750	TOTAL OF NEXT TOP 25 = 500	

YOUR ID40 SOCIAL JACK SCORE = 1,950

In Level 1 relationships, you barely have a relationship at all, but there is still *potential* for one. Your goal here would be to start to build vibrant exchanges that will result in mutually beneficial outcomes.

Then, as you move forward, you and your partners will start to experience small but significant successes such as new people coming into your network, or partners in your social team introducing you to new business or career opportunities.

But also realize that you need to approach Level 1 relationships thoughtfully. Not all potential team players will be on the same page when you begin this process.

For example, one of our new clients, John, was excited by the scoring method. He shared with me that he had begun talking to people in his network about it. He discovered that when he told one potential networking partner about this exercise and his intention to draft that partner onto his team, it caused their conversation to shift. But John went on, explaining further that he was exploring how they could help one another take their respective businesses to the next level. At that point, his potential partner responded, "Hang on a minute. You're out of rapport here.

It's a common tendency to get excited about something new and start talking to people who don't understand what you're doing. They may even be suspicious! Move slowly. We'll cover more about how to approach potential partners and what to say in the next couple of chapters. For now, spend your time assembling, selecting, and putting your draft picks on the planning sheet.

Power Move: *Organize your first draft picks.*

Go through your entire list of connections and start organizing your draft picks. Select their position within one of the four buckets: starters (5), bench players (10), practice squad (25), and farm team (everyone else).

FIRST Tryouts and Playing Your Players

Approaching others to recruit them into your network can be scary. But think of this time as a tryout for your team (your network.) This involves testing the proposed team you've assembled. Begin by learning at least one or two things about each player. In Social Jack we use the Player Sheets we created, but you can also create your own list.

As you proceed, make sure that you have a perceived relationship score for each potential networking partner. Then take time to learn more about each of your partners. Check out their LinkedIn profiles to find all kinds of useful information such as where they went to school, the jobs they've held, what others see as their top talents (through their recommendations), and even the social or nonprofit activities they care about.

You might prefer doing this on Facebook. Sometimes it's where you're most comfortable. Typically, you'll glean the best information if you go to where *they* reside digitally. It may be Instagram or Twitter.

Whatever source you research, the goal is to get a sense of who they are and what's important to them. To get the clearest picture and best results, you need to go to where they hang out on social media, which is not necessarily where you tend to spend a lot of time.

This will create a new level of sensitivity as you prepare to go on new appointments and are technically scouting new people. Do the same thing before you go into a meeting. This is the furthest thing from being creepy or stalky. It's done with the intent of gathering information that will help you more easily develop rapport.

You could begin by mentioning, "Oh, I noticed that you also are into martial arts" or "I read that you're a musician." As you bring these personal things up, people think, "Wow, he/she took the time to get to know me, to notice me. And yes, I did put that out there. I am a fan of the Seattle Seahawks."

Start by talking about something you have in common. That will lead to the development of a good conversation. If you don't have things in common, bring up something they're into that interests you. Maybe it's mountain climbing. You've never done that, but you find it exciting.

You already know that people love to talk about their passions—that's far from a secret. It's something we all do. Perhaps they love doing things with their family or posting about what their family members are up to.

That over-eager client I mentioned before was so ready to jump the gun before he had learned enough about this methodology. Another thing he immediately presumed was, "Oh, yeah, everybody wants to talk about family!" I took a deep breath and patiently replied, "No, they don't. You need to slow down and understand more about each individual."

He was trying to rush, making assumptions based on what he liked rather than finding out what the new connection/potential team player enjoys discussing. The basis for your tryouts lies within your players and who they are. Find this out before you have that first listening session.

Another real tryout occurs whenever you set an appointment, a conversation that's hopefully face-to-face. It could also be on Skype, Zoom, Facetime, or

Facebook—a forum where you can see the person. There are so many technologies where you can look somebody in the eyes. That's so important when building rapport and trust. Distance challenges might prevent meeting in person, but that's not the issue it was even in the early 2000s.

The main thing to remember is before you have that first meeting, take the time to get curious about them and see what they're all about.

This isn't about business at this stage. You're not seeking referrals yet. This initial time is about getting to know one another and building rapport and relationships. Your pure goal at this moment is to drive people up the scale with you, to that next relationship level.

You're driving them up to another relationship score, really working together. You want to begin the conversation with a lens focused entirely on being curious about them and the things that you've discovered. Your real goal is to take that relationship score up a notch every single time you talk to them.

Even if you feel you're already at a Level 5 with somebody, just keep going for more. A recent client told me that he thought we were at a Level 5. I considered that before answering, "You know, I think we're more at a Level 4. There are some things and places yet for us to go and discover."

Level 5 can't be a quick assumption. There still might be a lot of things you didn't know. You'll find yourself listening for these gems about someone. You'll be checked in. Even if you don't say it out loud, you'll think, "Oh, I never knew that about you." That's the magic. It's in the discovery. That's when you're human-to-human and saying, "Oh! I didn't know that about you! I've known you for ten years, and I had no idea!"

If you stay open to this, you'll find there are always more levels of discovery that you have with each relationship. It's important to appreciate that adventure and that discovery. This is where you get into playing your players and seeing and exploring the relationship with each one of them. You need to approach it casually when you begin doing it.

Meeting people professionally might be a new thing for you. They could be suspicious, especially if your previous connection has primarily been transactional rather than relational. If that's the case, they'll tend to think you're coming at them differently just to get a piece of business from them. This truly takes some effort, so be prepared to work at it.

It definitely demanded some effort on my part. For years, I was a numbers guy. I was always thinking, "I've got to get all these appointments, all these deals. I need to get so many proposals out." Being in sales creates a lot of pressure like that. When you're doing this relationship scoring, you'll find it's a delicate balance of personal and business interactions.

The goal here is getting into the next piece, which I call the Referral Machine. Without getting too "fast and furious" here, I want you to understand that the goal in doing this Relationship Level scoring is that it works its way up to a level of permission. When people get to a Level 3 with you, you'll notice that you've hit a point where they have the relationships with the right people in their network who you want to meet.

This is the part of our exercise when we get into social selling and appointment setting. This leads to a high level of activity. As you're driving yourself to network and to conferences and getting into new hubs, you'll reach a point where there's a whole new level of exploration that's just beautiful and amazing for you.

How will you know for sure you've arrived there? You start hearing people ask you things like, "How can I help you? Or "I have someone that needs to meet you" without you even needing to make a request. This is when you've reached a whole new level of play. When people begin to embrace their relationship with you, that means you're climbing up that relationship score and they're genuinely asking, "How can I help you?"

I still get overwhelmed with the number of people who ask me this. In fact, it took a while of coaching work for me to accept it, being the street guy on my own and alone. Sure, it was lonely, but I was used to it. At least it was a known factor, and in some ways, it was strangely comfortable. Because of that background, I felt guilty for whatever reason. I was wired that way. I believed that I wasn't deserving of someone's help, and I didn't trust it for a long time.

This could be a whole different journey for whoever you are and however you're wired. Just make sure that once you've built your social team and developed a level of trust, these partners will honestly want to help you.

When they do make that offer, allow yourself to feel the genuine nature of it, the care and intention for mutuality and reciprocity. When you do, then you'll be able to respond along the lines of, "Well, as a matter of fact, I saw that you had so-and-so in your network. Would you be able to make a referral for me?"

Honestly, when I've gotten to a Level 3, 4, or 5 with someone with the intent of building relationship, I've never had anyone turn me down when I've asked for a referral. In fact, when the relationships get to a Level 4 or 5, you have people who'll just bring you referrals automatically. This becomes the true Referral Machine I mentioned.

Always work on your relationship first, and then on getting referrals. This book is not about social selling. There's plenty out there in the world about social selling, appointment setting, and how to ask for referrals. As I mentioned earlier, the Power Moves shared in this book will take you to those places. Spending 20-minutes a day to build relationships will add up over time. Soon you'll hear your networking partners asking, "How can I help you?" At this point, your social team is firing on all cylinders.

As you continue to optimize your team, the first key part will become your comfort zone, which means you'll be tempted to stop scouting and drafting. Remember: you will never stop scouting and drafting. As things unfold, you'll realize and recognize that some players just don't want to play. It doesn't feel right. It's not a good relationship. It's time to draft someone else. As part of your social-teaming endeavors, you want to make sure you're driving this to a level of mutual satisfaction.

We get into a celebration at the end of this book, and I want you to celebrate all along the way. Celebrate and be grateful for the network that you've built up to this moment. Once again, there's no shame if you feel like your team is crap right now. The point is there are good relationships in there. The good news is that they're a pathway to the next best team that you'll ever have, always and consistently.

Power Move: *Schedule your first tryouts.*

Get into your first tryouts. Get into a level of play with your teammates when you book that appointment or Skype call. Make sure that you're looking in their eyes. Let them know that you care about them and are in this relationship for the long haul. Your goal is to drive that relationship score up one more notch—for you and for them—so it's for the both of you.

Hold Two Tryouts a Day

Once you have established solid networking relationships, a good rule of thumb to follow is to wait about three or four months before you share what you're doing with scouting, drafting, and so forth. The primary goal is to take your current team and play two players a day. Just two, in the fashion that's been laid out here. Make sure that every day when it pops up on your calendar, you're moving down your list of players. Really enjoy playing your two players a day as you work your way through the entire list of forty.

Once you've done that, start playing two people a day from your farm team. These are people way off the sheet, right? They're not part of your initial team, but they have potential. They may or may not turn out to be teammates for you, but the awareness you gain can be amazing.

This is a simple cyclic rotation. Some people prefer to use CRM while playing their two a day, while others like doing this on Excel spreadsheets. Our Social Jack platform offers free worksheets that you can download if you wish.

The main thing is for you to see the power in fitting this in with how you track people and track your systems. Every day, two tryouts and just track your results. If you miss a day, you miss a day. Just get up the next day, and it's draft day. One more thing: HAVE FUN! It's about having fun as you're building relationships and generating a lifetime of referrals.

A Favor

My last request in this chapter is incredibly important to me. Please, once you have benefitted from learning this approach, teach this to others. Teach it to your family, your children, your friends, those you care about. This process is something we've used in our Social Jack curriculum to help college students get early job placements and amazing internships.

Building a powerful social team and network—nothing else can take its place. Science estimates that 72% of the Earth is made up of water. Personally, I believe there is a bountiful percentage of amazing connections and relationships on the planet. They're ours to have, nurture, develop, and grow.

Relationships are one thing we can all have in abundance. We need never live in scarcity by being alone, neither in relationship or connections. I spent far too many years of my life feeling and being alone. This chapter was done from the sheer passion that I never want people around me to go through feeling alone, unconnected, to lose the gift of relationship.

I ask that you please make sure you teach this to those you care about. Make sure that you practice it each day. When you do, I promise you will always be rich with relationships—in business, in life, forever.

YOUR *FIRST* LAUNCH
into Social Media

What we call "stepping onto the dance floor" is getting to that point where you're willing to put yourself into social media. It's one thing to have your story done. It's another to have your profile done. But it's surprising to people who know and are familiar with social media how different it becomes when you talk about doing it on a business or professional level. Some people embrace it, trust it, and follow exactly what we say and do. Others just come away with complete fear.

Take Tom Meyer, an executive and part owner of Centrust Bank in Chicago. I've known him for a long time. Being in commercial banking, he deals with a lot of businesses and is a natural networker. His top-producing numbers year after year prove his skill level. As with anybody, certain things come up for him. They ask him, "Does this really work? Is it going to be worth my time? I want to make sure I don't look stupid." A lot of initial fears arise.

When dealing with Tom, we told him, "This is going to be great! You're already an amazing networker. People are going to respond to you." Not long after he started posting leadership articles, we saw an immediate engagement. Once Tom started doing this, not only did he start to see remarkable results, but he also started to get business from it. It happened so fast that he almost became addicted to the fact that this does work—you can get business from it.

Once Tom got in the game, he was so over the top with it that he spoke to the president of Centrust. Jim McMahon, the president, also has this amazing mindset. In fact, we just did a press release on the bank's transformation. After Tom got connected and moved to his next level, I trained some executives and others in his bank. Next thing you know, we're training his entire staff.

Now everybody's playing, and what's funny is that Tom is one of the top bankers trending on Twitter, of all places! And not for just one thing, but every week their bank is trending, as are their individual people. And they are a single location community bank.

So now they're all out on the dance floor. You've been to weddings where they'll call certain people out on the dance floor. It starts with one couple, then they add another, and before long there are 5, 6, 7, 10 of them. They're all dancing out there, and that's what it should be like. It should be fun. It should be engaging.

In fact, one of the bank people even remarked, "Oh, and it's fun!" That's our goal—to get to a point where it's so natural and engaging that connecting is fun. The fact that it also generates fantastic results is the icing on the cake.

Get Your Team Ready to Play, *FIRST*

Just as Tom Meyer was able to achieve digital business influence online, you can do it, too. Start by asking, "Who are the easiest people to play (a.k.a. network with you) on your team? Who do you currently know and trust the most? Are they ready to engage? If yes, then which of those potential players has a growth mindset and is ready to create those mutually beneficial opportunities?

Make sure they're on social media. This is about finding those who actively want to network with you. They should also know you're going to start posting and promoting them online.

A typical next question is, "Great. So how do I do that? How do I tell them?" First look online. Do they post content on LinkedIn or anywhere you are connected? Start engaging with them first! Then if they have little or nothing, time to pick up the phone.

Do this by calling up your potential team players and talking with them. You can say, for example, "'Hey, listen, I'm new at social media as it applies to business and need your help. I'm going to be posting some thought-leadership articles, and I would love it if you guys would *Like* or *Comment,* and engage on those."

We always ask our clients to teach someone else what they've learned because they learn by teaching others. This gives them a kick start in adopting these new social connection skills. It's perfectly okay to let people on your team know that you're going to be on social media, and this is a new thing for you. Tell them you might be hesitant about it, or you're nervous about it, and you want some allies. You want some people who will chime in and help you out.

It's about making sure that you notify your team. Be sure you tell them where you'll be posting as well as when so they can be on the lookout. Just ask them to *Like* or *Comment* on a few things that you have going out there so that you don't feel that you're operating "alone" in this new venture. It's similar to coordinating a meeting with someone face-to-face at an event.

You're creating a practice of energy around your conversation. Again, this is no different than being at a live event when you walk in and everybody you know is standing around, talking in a circle. You just walk up and jump into that conversation, right? The power of social reach, covered earlier in this book, is that you get a dynamic every time there's an engagement. Roughly 8,000 people have the potential to see somewhere in the news feed that you're engaging.

Whether it's in someone else's network or yours, the average visibility reach is about 8,000, even though some will tell you it's way more or way less. We won't get into the algorithm war here. There's so much content circulating out there that it's around 8,000 by two degrees of that network.

As you see this, every time there's an engagement, not only do you get that connection and that feeling of doing a good job and succeeding, you have the energy of others seeing that post. You're inviting others to *Like*, *Comment*, and engage. That's why you want to make sure your team is there so that you feel comfortable and good about the process. Getting your team's feedback is invaluable.

Power Move: *Get Team Feedback.*

Ask for feedback from your team. Request that they make genuine comments and honestly contribute. Get your team ready to play first, then you're ready to move on to the next steps.

FIRST Five Fears

My work team and I always talk about feelings. Human beings are born with primal fears, that "Fight, Flight or Freeze" impulse. There are a couple of different fears that show up when we're working in social media. It's part of being human—just being who we truly are.

Fear # 1: *"I'm Not Good Enough"*

Among the biggest of these is the fear of inadequacy. Again, some of these fears originate from the way we were raised. Some are so deeply buried within us that we don't even realize we have them. They're tied into our conditioned self-esteem, even apart from social media.

Social media creates a level of anxiety that "I'm going to look bad" or "I'm not going to do it right" or "I'll look stupid." People have this fear of being inadequate, of not receiving enough *Likes* or *Comments*.

We begin getting our clients through this by finding out what their fears and beliefs are. A lot of times that will come out in their story. That's a cue for us to say, "Okay, when we go to have them out on the dance floor, we're going to have to deal with a couple of these things. We know that this is coming."

Next, we warm them up and get them relaxed about having conversations. We'll do some role playing. We'll sit with them and go through when we're posting and ask, "What would you say when doing this? How would you feel when you say that?" We also lead by example. Here, we act as if we are them and allow them to shadow us in the process. Then we hand the keys back to them. This can take a few rounds. We work a bit slowly at first to make sure that they get it. Then we release them to try it on their own.

Fear # 2: *FOMO*

Another fear that comes up in epidemic proportions is the Fear Of Missing Out (FOMO). It's a contributing factor to people jumping on board with social media early on. But FOMO is also to blame for why certain people choose to represent themselves in phony or fake ways. Rather than show up as their authentic selves, they show up as who they thought the world wants them to be, how they should portray themselves to live up to others' expectations to avoid judgment. It becomes a push/pull involvement.

There was this thing of "Oh, my gosh! I have to login; I have to post. I have to connect. I have to grab more friends. I have to grab some connections." This happens because people had this fear that they would miss out.

We would rather have people build a smaller, more targeted network and be micro-influencers, rather than try to pull out all the stops and be instantaneously connected to everyone. Anyone who attempts to become a macro-influencer to a large non-relevant audience is missing out on a lot. It's far more important that they learn to be in relationships in a better way with the people they're connected to, or the network that they're connected to. It's about making that shift and developing a relationship with that network.

We help them learn to release the worry that they're not enough. That's why we create a "network map" that shows exactly what to do on which days with suggested times. We make it very simple, very easy. Everything we do is 20-minutes a day or under. You're connecting and engaging with the intent to forge relationships, much like at an event.

The goal here is to accept that if you occasionally miss a day, that's okay. You can come back tomorrow. Don't freak out. Don't stress out if you don't hit every mark on the schedule. Be intentional about being with your network in relationships. We would rather have you login less and go a little deeper with select people on your social team than try to connect to everybody at a shallow level. It's about "being," not "doing." This is

where the whole thing unmasks that FOMO is not real. It's an illusion.

For instance, you'll read a post or hear somebody say, "Wow! Did you see what so-and-so put online?" You get this anxiety that you weren't there. You can always go there and take a look when you have time, so just relax. Rather than buying into the panic, just respond with something like "No, I didn't. But great! Thanks for telling me. I'll check it out soon." A million things are posted every single day. You're never going to see everything. It's important to be okay with that. Release that FOMO once and for all.

Fear #3: *No Time*

Another fear that we find present with many executives is the fear of not having enough time to participate in social media. We came up with the 20-minutes-a-day strategy to overcome that fear of limited time. "I don't have enough time. I'm overbooked. I'm double-booked." This has always been a thing of mine: "I'm so busy, I'm so busy." It's like the March Hare in *Alice in Wonderland,* running around frantically saying, "I'm late, I'm late! For a very important date, no time to say hello, goodbye, I'm *late!*" That was me for so long, just rushing to that next thing.

I was never present. Don't be the hare. Slow down, plot out, and do less. Do better, go deeper, and be more present where you are rather than worrying about where you're not.

The time thing is one of those issues over which we have control. That's why we say, "Book your 20 minutes a day, and pick the best time of day for you." Power Moves are intentionally designed to not overwhelm you. To this end, we created them in increments of one, three, or five-minute activities. This formatting helps generate results in simple, hyper-focused movements so you can pack them into 20 minutes a day or less. As a result, you accelerate your success and don't get overwhelmed.

If for some reason you can't do it on a certain day, it's like an appointment that you can move around as needed. It's about holding the awareness that your event is going on, and that it's okay to attend that event at 6 a.m. or noon, whenever it works for you. Don't take a lot of time with this. It's so easy to get lost and overwhelmed by the glut of information out there. Remember it's about the people not the content!

We don't want you in there for an hour or more. Some people say, "I do an hour-and-a-half a day in social media." I'm astounded and ask, "What on earth do you DO for an hour and a half a day? Better yet, what do you get out of it?" Granted, some people have legitimate reasons. For example, they're in a sales role, and it makes good sense for them to prospect and dig that deep. But for most of us, generating one decent high-level referral or appointment every five minutes— that's four good appointments per 20-minute time period. That's pretty darned good for most of us.

Fear # 4: *Fear of Failure*

This could be on a personal level or a business level. Often, it's both. We see this a lot at the personal level on Facebook, more on the professional level with LinkedIn. They feel if they post the wrong thing, they're either going to harm relationships or themselves in some way, or harm their entire career or their business.

I've worked most of my career coming through the ranks, starting at Merrill Lynch. Then building a company, winding up in a CPA firm, and building another company.

I also have worked for decades within the financial and banking space and understand the fear of compliance that comes down from HR and the legal and compliance departments. They put fear in everybody. The first thing out of most people's mouths is, "I can't do that," even before they know if they can or not. That stems from this fear of failing at their job, of getting fired.

I've been there, done that, and want to share that part of my story with you here. It's a bit of a flashback, but it's a viable example of what living and working in fear can bring forth.

When You Play out of Fear, You set Yourself up for a Fall

At nineteen, I finally made a clean break from my past and was living and working in downtown Chicago at Merrill Lynch. I was working with and learning more about computers. I thought everything was in alignment for a fresh start, but then a whole new level of bad influence surfaced.

All kinds of toxic things were going on at the company. I didn't know who to trust. Many times I felt very much alone, having no one with whom I could share my deepest thoughts and fears. This was the 1980s, and it wasn't just the salaries that were high. Cocaine was a regular presence at business meetings.

My initial happiness about escaping the dark side of my youth was rapidly disappearing with the realization that I was now in another negative space. I found myself roped into what I came to call "hostage partying." My boss would pull me into one party after another. I became his go-to "party guy." He regularly booked hotel rooms complete with booze, drugs, hookers, and lots of people eager to partake in all of it. Many of my friends and colleagues where also caught up in this.

I grew to dread the words, "Dean, go set up the hotel room." That involved lots of sleazy components. I became an unwilling-yet-active participant in the dirty underbelly of the corporate world. I was forced to play my part by pulling all of this stuff together whenever I was asked. He knew I owed him big time for the job, and he probably thought, "Ah, he's just a naïve young kid. He won't mind doing some of the dirty work."

More than once I thought, "Well, this is a shitty deal. I thought I was networking my way out of it, but now I'm just in a bigger street gang. Playing at a different level is all it is. I'm in a white-collar gang."

Because I found myself in the middle of all that, I thought, "Oh, my God. This is what the whole world's like." That became my view of corporate America...of the world.

I was going to a trade school, the Chicago Computer Learning Center, at night, and working hard at Merrill Lynch. I met new friends in technology and worked to keep branching out to new networks.

Things finally reached a point where the top brass got wind of my boss's underground activities. He was fired and busted for embezzling vast sums of money and a host of other illegal stuff. Not surprisingly, everyone associated with him got fired right along with him. I'll never forget the feeling of being set up to be fired. It's like the devastating feeling of coming home to discover your house has been robbed. It's an outright violation, and it cuts deep.

I was doing everything by the book, trying to be the best employee possible. Yet those now in power called me on the carpet and flung a bunch of lies at me. "Look, Dean, this was done wrong, and you screwed that up." I probably had that deer-in-the-headlights look as I protested, "But that wasn't even my responsibility. I didn't work on that at all." Their cold, dead eyes looked through me as they pointed out, "Well, your initials are right here, so we have no other choice than to let you go." I was guilty by association, and they were cleaning house. No social team left here!

I'm now grateful that I was let go because it freed me up to move forward and start my own first company. But my fear-induced compliance with all those seedy activities was what set me up for a fall before things got back on track. It's sad that we've bought into this fear-based environment.

That's why I love working with a bank like Centrust, financial-services firms, or insurance firms. Their leaders go through our training, and then step up and say, "No, we're going to embrace this. We'll train our people what to do and tell them this is no different than a code of conduct when representing us in public or at an event. You'll just behave in a confident, relaxed fashion after we've trained you on how to have good, deep, and engaging conversations for relationships." They are the true digital thought leaders in our world!

This is where failure is within your control. If the only fear you have is that your company may not give you the proper training, then that's why we created Social Jack. It gives people a place to go whether they have very little time or money. They know they can always go there and find ways to make sure that they are successful and won't fail. And if their company does not comply, then they now have the skills to find a "growth mindset" organization, be happier and make more.

Fear #5: *Fear of Social Judgment, Looking Bad, Bad Taste, or Bad Associations*

Through my years of teaching and coaching in building digital business influence, I've observed that many people have a negative image of themselves. I refer to this as the "fear of bad taste." The idea here is that certain people's posts make you just squirm when you see them. You know who they are. Due to whatever makes you uncomfortable, you might choose to unfriend them, or you hide their posts.

The first thing you think is, "Oh, man! I hope my network doesn't see that I'm connected to this person because I'll become guilty by association." We start believing that person's opinions are going to make us look bad. I have people who connect to me even if we aren't friends in some cases, yet they still tag me on posts and rants. I ask them to stop, and they don't. I simply unfriend and block them if necessary (you know who you are). Typically, three strikes and you're off the team!

If you're not familiar with Spotify, it's one of the first social networks built around music. When it first came out, people were afraid that others would see what kind of music they listen to and make judgments about them. It's true! There was fear of social judgment— just around music! We still have the same judgments around Facebook and other formats with our posting, and what we're going to put out there. "Oh! Will people take that the wrong way?"

We must be careful. Once you become trained in conversation and make sure that you're a thought leader who's putting the right things out there, you'll get comfortable in your own skin. You'll know what's good or bad. Think about it this way: it's no different than if you say something during an in-person discussion, like sitting around the lunch table with other people. What would you say when you were at work? How would you address this? No different than the Code of Conduct agreements we have signed over the decades.

We try to work with folks so they can overcome their primary fears. Those are the reasons that it's so important for people to embrace that first. I know from my own training that it's about embracing my fears and knowing that every time I feel fear, it presents an opportunity for me to train, to know more, do better, try harder.

Embracing fear presents so much opportunity for learning and growth. Talk about it with a friend, colleague, trainer, or coach. Use your social team. They have the same feelings. Rather than running away, hiding, or just not doing it, work through the fear! Don't remain shut down and let your competitor take all your people who are talking to others.

There's nothing worse than when somebody says, "Oh, I forgot you did that, or I would have called you," or "I just hired so-and-so to do this." It's something you could have helped with, but they didn't remember your skills. That's what we don't want for you.

It seems like I just created another fear in that statement, right? The fear of not doing it. But I don't want you to do it from FOMO, or from any fear. I want you to do it from the desire and intent to succeed and to help others succeed as well. When that's your motivation, you will soon see positive shifts all around you.

Power Move: *Write down your first primary fears, the fears that came up while reading this chapter*

If you have big fears, write those down as well. This is the first step in helping you to embrace, and then overcome them. We call this "name it to tame it." When you have the fear, embrace it, talk about it, and look for the opportunity and what you need to know so you're not afraid anymore. Always use it as a learning opportunity.

FIRST Get an Accountability Partner or Coach

As our clients first fill out their profiles, there's a section called Peer Review where they identify somebody they trust, who they can count on. I always like the buddy system. There's co-accountability. Even if they don't hire a coach but just have someone who is going to hold them accountable, that can work out extremely well. It should be someone you trust, someone who you're unafraid to tell the truth (a true Level 5 relationship).

Choose one or two people that you know are going to stick with you and follow through. Create a mutual accountability support system. It's one of the most powerful tools you'll have to keep you on track.

Neuroscience has proven that because of the way our brains are wired, it takes a minimum of 21 days

of consistent repetition to create a new habit and/
or thought system for success. That's why so many
motivational gurus have 30-day programs. They're
hoping you'll stay on course with it for at *least* 21 days!
Make sure your accountability coach(es) commit to a
21-day minimum schedule with you.

**Power Move: *Choose an accountability partner/
coach.***

Choose an accountability partner or coach as
described above and begin working with them now.
Keep it simple—start small. Focus on only the next
thing you need to work on, and don't think about
everything at once. Stop, text them now and setup an
in person or virtual Skype coffee.

Your *FIRST* Truth Talk

Posting your first real thought leadership post is also
your first Truth Talk. A Truth Talk is when you're not
holding back while speaking with somebody. You're
being authentic, genuine, and expressing your feelings.
You're telling somebody exactly how you feel about
something. There's a balance between doing this and
making sure you're responsible with your feelings in
doing it. You want to make sure that you're telling
people that it's okay to disagree with something, that
it's okay to take a position that's different than yours.

We say don't take political and religious positions
(remember the *code of conduct*). These are things best
kept out of your thought-leadership postings. When it
comes to business, if you strongly believe that all great

leaders do X, Y, and Z, state that you believe that. Get dynamic with your thoughts.

You're accomplishing two things this way: showcasing your own unique narrative and building genuine rapport. That will evolve into getting a little deeper and a little more emotional. Here others *feel* part of the conversation and they can relate. This is what invites them to talk to you and engage in giving you feedback and comments.

This is when you start to get real. You're not just going through the motions of pushing content out there. Rather, you are starting a purposeful conversation. Understand that before you post what we call your first *Truth Talk,* practice conversations with someone—an accountability partner—someone you know, in person. Get their reactions. As you get more comfortable with these deeper conversations, you'll find what feels appropriate to put online.

It may also help to record and play these talks back. Don't be too hard on yourself. This is not a time to beat yourself up. It's a time to learn and grow and make improvements. We always hear ourselves differently and more critically than others do. That is why you want to do this with an accountability partner.

Have your accountability partner or coach listen to your first Truth Talk. They will give you accurate feedback in terms of what that feels like. This is something that we love to do. People realize how they sound and get a reflection from the other person.

Power Move: *Schedule and book the Truth Talk with your accountability partner or coach.*

***FIRST* Reactions from Your Team**

At Social Jack we like to remind folks to "forgive people, for they don't know what they do sometimes." What we mean is that inevitably when we ask people to support us—help us, to be there for us—sometimes they just won't show up. It's not because they don't want to. Perhaps they're dealing with their own fear and may have said, "Yes, I do want to get on LinkedIn, and I'll watch out for your stuff. I'll help you," but then they don't do it. That leads to you feeling that you have been abandoned or left alone.

Naturally, you feel hurt when that happens. You wind up with some anxiety. Your fears get magnified around the fact that nobody cares, that you're alone. But that's not true! They just may be dealing with their own stuff.

The best thing you can do when you hit this bump is to say, "Hey! I noticed you hadn't liked or commented on any of my posts, and I just wanted to see if you have some suggestions, or did you just get busy and forget?" I guarantee you, 99 percent of the time, they'll say, "Oh, my gosh, no. I forgot." You may run into that completely honest 1% that will admit they don't post that often and weren't exactly sure what to do. You now have an opportunity to get both sides of this.

NOTE: There are also a lot of new algorithms that prevent some of those in your network from seeing your posting activity. The activities I'm suggesting in this chapter will also help your content get visible online.

You'll find that you have people who *Like* and *Comment*. It's vital to thank them. This should be an ongoing practice. We even have the *Gratitude Post*, where we thank people for their comments and participation. We thank them for feedback and make sure we're giving, receiving, and staying engaged. All of the above should become a regular part of your relationship building that takes your success to the next level.

As you get the first reactions from your team, deal with this in a relationship fashion. When someone forgets, stay in clear communication with them by asking, "Did you actually forget, or did you not understand my request?" Talk and work through this, just as you would with any relationship endeavor.

When you're thanking people in the *Comments* section of your posts, be sure to also shoot them a text message. (e.g., "I really appreciate you helping me out with your feedback. Thanks again for your connection.")

It's funny that, I have people I did this with seven, eight, nine years ago who still show up. I make sure I go out of my way to find their content, and go back and *Like* and *Comment* for them. I sometimes share their content so they feel cared for in connection and relationship.

Many times, no big surprise, I get unsolicited referrals from these people. People just show up. At first, it may feel like they came out of nowhere, but they emerged from that early effort. Make sure you understand the reactions from your team and that you're in a relationship with them as you deal with those issues.

Power Move: *Thank people or communicate with people who may not have replied yet.*

Your *FIRST* Score

Ideally, there will always be magical moments that come out of our work with clients and in their work within their networks. Since we're running a team environment, the biggest thing that people acknowledge are the wins that come out of this. We look at a score with many things. We talked about connecting to your team, having your team help you as part of this, and putting your first post and first content online.

When people start to react, you'll be surprised at who surfaces. Many of them will wind up asking you to get together, have an appointment, or be reminded of what you do. You'll automatically get a referral from this exercise. One of the coolest aspects of this is making sure that you acknowledge that. Watch for those referrals and how they come about.

These may arrive via your direct messages or your inbox, depending upon which platform you're in. They could come by email, text message, or in the form of an actual conversation that's happening online.

Structurally, as you're putting content out there, keep following and connecting to other thought leaders. As you're commenting and speaking the truth as it applies to that content, you're going to start seeing signals from people who want to talk to you.

On the flipside, watch out for any fear that may crop up. Know that it's okay for you to see people who surface. Go and approach them directly for that meeting.

We always like to make sure that this is the first part of understanding the power that you have and the simple moves that you make.

Power Move: *Tune into those magic moments*.

Focus on being tuned in as those magic moment connections surface for you so that you can reap the rewards. Many times, that's just reconnecting to somebody, simply having an appointment, or going to the point of generating a referral out of your initial activity. That's what we mean by the *first* score.

FIRST MEANINGFUL
Conversations

This chapter reminds me of training my son Jackson, who has been working with me since the age of ten. He would work local networking events with me where I would pay him twenty-five cents a business card to collect and enter items into a spreadsheet, but only if he could remember and document two things about what the company did. Any personal info about that person would be a bonus.

He would have to have a deeper conversation with the individual in order to do this, and to this day (10 years later) he goes deep in every conversation in which he engages, both in person and online.

FIRST Realization of Engagement Levels

Look at online networking as being similar to attending a live networking event, but even better. Consider that right in front of you is a profile of each person with lots of useful information to start an engaging exchange.

For example, you can learn things such as whether you went to schools that were similar, or you played the same sports; where your connections work now, and did before; the type of volunteering they might be doing, and so on. Glean what they are most interested in based on the groups they have joined and use some of the many points of connection to break the ice as you reach out to start a conversation that builds engagement.

Available on social media platforms (LinkedIn, Instagram, Facebook, and so on) is a *Like* option. In fact, Facebook went to the next level and included emojis so you could love, dislike, or even be angry or sad at something—a whole gamut of feelings. In effect, they offer you the opportunity to share different levels of engagement by giving you an easy button. But in our world, an easy button doesn't quite cut it when you're working on building relationships. Granted, it's good filler, but it's not valuable when it comes to taking a connection to the next level.

Watch out for taking the easy route and simply *Liking* people's posts or *Comments* or hitting the little heart button on Instagram. I see people scanning and doing that. It drives me crazy. It harkens back to FOMO. They feel like they're with all those people and connecting with them, yet it's not truly with the intent of developing a genuine and authentic relationship.

As part of building engagement, slow down. Make sure that you're not just *Liking* everything and then jumping onto the next post that catches your eye. This is the equivalent of walking into a room and saying, "Oh, I like your tie. I like your hat. I like your jacket." Here, you are not engaging but simply making small talk that goes nowhere. We call these types of people "Likeaholics" because they are so afraid of missing out that they *Like* pretty much...everything.

To build a strong network with the purpose of becoming a thought leader, your goal should be to create rich conversations that build value between you and those with whom you network. This is how you successfully build your business.

Whatever your initial goals were, you already know who your targets are. Then go online and take the time to read what your target connections are posting, and then *Comment* with your own insights. These comment add additional value to their thoughts which they will appreciate, especially if you take the time to do this regularly.

Another value-added tip is to pick ideas out of their articles that you find most interesting and share them with your network. Now you have added value to your network as well as your target's network. Eventually, as you connect and offer your insights, you will *engage* with your targets, turning your contributions into conversations.

Then as you begin to build *conversation bridges,* you will also develop relationships that will help you become known as being someone they want to hear from more often. As you take time to offer any unique insights you have, you should also start be seen as a thought leader. These *deeper conversations* are what every thought leader online hopes will occur. You want

to go from just unconsciously "liking" the comments of others but also consciously tuning in and becoming an important part of these conversations.

Billy Dexter's book, *Making Your Net Work: Mastering The Art and Science of Career and Business Networking*, clearly outlines how to stay "awake in the network." As a partner in corporate board placement in one of the top executive search firms in the world, Billy's done that at the mastery level. He's awake in his networks because he takes the time to see what his network partners are saying and, over time, notices the things that most matter to them. As a result, others welcome the comments he shares with them. That's the goal—to be a welcome source of online wisdom.

If you choose to follow the suggested time limit of engaging for 20 minutes each day on social media, you'll also need to select a certain number of people to follow (your social team). By doing this, you will get to a point where you see them in a value-added way. You will become awake in the network. Billy's co-author and my friend, Melissa G Wilson, regularly states, "People constantly confuse activity with accomplishment."

That's why it's important to keep your focus on adding value through connecting regularly online with your social team. To recap, this is your team of 40. That's your 5 Starters, 10 Bench Players, and 25 Practice Squad members.

Start following them, but also put them on Google Alerts. By doing this, you will get alerts each time they post or are mentioned online, first. This will give you much more impact online as you can respond quickly. Additionally, this will show others in your social team's network that you are socially savvy and quite astute online. Remember we are rising to a new level of consciousness and "being" here.

You can also use the auto-notification system that your various social media platforms use (your CRM system) so that you get an alert whenever they post rather than spending time searching online for their information. Once you do that, you're essentially creating a lift above all the noise. You're also raising the quality of your network.

Additionally you will receive notifications about all your team members rather than drowning in the internet's sea of TMI (Too Much Information). If you stop to think about it, if each team member has ten or more clients also engaging online, you're positioning yourself to gain an introduction and build business with their extended network.

Integrating the 20-minute process into your daily schedule will ensure your success online but will also have tangible results in your face-to-face networking and your business success.

TEAM SHEET

Following is an example of the form we use at Social Jack to build your team.

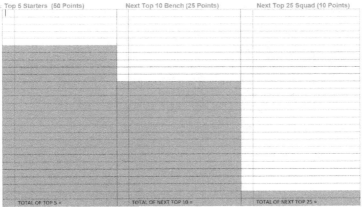

MY IDEAL 40 Team – SOCIAL JACK SCORING VERSION

Top 5 Starters (50 Points)	Next Top 10 Bench (25 Points)	Next Top 25 Squad (10 Points)
TOTAL OF TOP 5 =	TOTAL OF NEXT TOP 10 =	TOTAL OF NEXT TOP 25 =

YOUR ID40 SOCIAL JACK TEAM SCORE = _____

And following is a sample of one of our team sheets filled out:

MY IDEAL 40 – ID40 – SOCIAL JACK SCORING VERSION - EXAMPLE

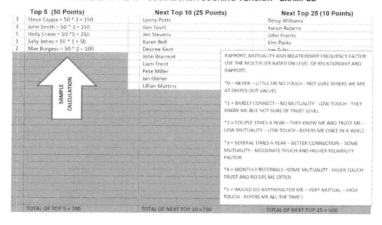

Top 5 (50 Points)	Next Top 10 (25 Points)	Next Top 25 (10 Points)
3	Steve Cappa = 50 * 3 = 150	Lenny Potts	Betsy Williams
3	John Smith = 50 * 3 = 150	Ken Tuvill	Karen Rubens
5	Holly Crane = 50 *5 = 250	Jim Stevens	John Franks
1	Sally Johns = 50 * 1 = 50	Karen Bell	Kim Parks
2	Max Burgess = 50 * 2 = 100	Desiree Kent	Low Zube
		John Warrent	RAPPORT, MUTUALITY AND RELATIONSHIP FREQUENCY FACTOR: USE THE MULTIPLIER BASED ON LEVEL OF RELATIONSHIP AND RAPPORT.
		Liam Trent	
		Pete Miller	
		Jan Olsher	*0 – NEVER – LITTLE OR NO TOUCH - NOT SURE WHERE WE ARE AT (WIPES OUT VALUE)
		Lillian Martins	
			*1 = BARELY CONNECT – NO MUTUALITY - LOW TOUCH - THEY KNOW ME BUT NOT SURE OF TRUST LEVEL
			*2 = COUPLE TIMES A YEAR – THEY KNOW ME AND TRUST ME – LOW MUTUALITY – LOW TOUCH - REFERS ME ONCE IN A WHILE
			*3 = SEVERAL TIMES A YEAR – BETTER CONNECTION - SOME MUTUALITY - MODERATE TOUCH AND HIGHER RELIABILITY FACTOR
			*4 = MONTHLY REFERRALS –SOME MUTUALITY - HIGER TOUCH - TRUST AND REFERS ME OFTEN
			*5 = WOULD DO ANYTHING FOR ME – VERY MUTUAL – HIGH TOUCH - REFERS ME ALL THE TIME!)
TOTAL OF TOP 5 = 700	TOTAL OF NEXT TOP 10 =750	TOTAL OF NEXT TOP 25 = 500

YOUR ID40 SOCIAL JACK SCORE = 1,950

Whenever needed, scout for new team players. Then once you connect, determine if they are a fit for your team. Every day, also play two members from your current team.

SCOUT, DRAFT, BUILD, AND PLAY

Social Jack™ Scouting and Drafting Game Plan - Score Card		Monday	Tuesday	Wednesday	Thursday	Friday	TOTAL
2 Old / 2 New	20 per week	1 Old Steve Smith	Barb Loggins	Jason Parker	Jon Paul	Greg Jarre	
		2 Old Karen Jones	Bob Cheque	Angie Phillips	Steve Balich	Joyce Kagan	
		1 New Steve Terry	Gail Ludeweiss	Holly Barker	Marc Dixon	Manny O	
		2 New Bill Smith	Ron Miller	Shawn Kent	Rebecca Considine	Ken Shaunessy	
		4	4	4	4	4	20
Face to Face Meetings	10 per week	1 Dean Jones	Tim Jensen	Paul David	Cherly Bellavia	Shelley Long	
		2 Kevin Lock	Karen Prep	Susan Maggino	Scott Morris	Joe Mazzaro	
		3					
		2	2	2	2	2	10

Remember to follow the "two old, two new" rule as you cycle through connecting your team members.

Power Move: *Be conscious of your engagement levels.*

Get your alerts on your team players and then watch and purposefully and meaningfully engage with them online.

The Power of *FIRST* Engagement

First engagement, mentioned earlier in the *Stepping Out on the Dance Floor* section of the book, happens when you find your team members online and interact with them in some type of value-added, reciprocal way. Maybe the reciprocity is that you engage with their content—those people/team members that helped you out by commenting on your *first* post. Make sure you take the time to read their posts or articles and get to know who they are by what they're writing. Commit to making deep, thoughtful comments about you read that they share.

Take time to acknowledge your team members often by telling them that you've learned something from them or were deeply moved by something they wrote. It's good to let them know how their content helped you or your company, that you appreciate them and the content they shared helped you grow your business to the next level.

Acknowledging your team players regularly is an important relationship builder. Think about the times you've posted something you spent a lot of time developing. You believed it was a great piece of content that you wrote, but it didn't get any *Likes* or *Comments*. You would have appreciated even one person from your network recognizing that you were offering something of value.

In our classes we ask our clients, "What's the primary emotion that you experience when you don't get any attention – when no one reaches out? You started an amazing conversation. You even went further and wrote an article about it and shared it online. But nobody's *Liking* or *Commenting* on it. What does that feel like?" They respond, "Well, I feel rejected and abandoned," or "I feel hurt," or "I'm sad," or "I feel like the things I'm doing are not worthy." All kinds of feelings come up.

We then ask, "What happens when you get a whole bunch of *Likes* and *Comments*?" For example, the overwhelming famous birthday posts on Facebook. Heck, you even have complete strangers wishing you Happy Birthday. (They are part of your network; you just don't know them yet.) Their faces light up, and they say, "Extreme joy! I feel affirmed, connected, and attached." As you come into these moments where you're providing that for somebody else, it feeds you as well. You feel special, and wanted, and supported.

Power Move: *Stop the small talk—go deeper with your conversation.*

   Don't be content to simply make small talk with your network. Go into deep talk. Make sure that you're connecting with that person for them, as well as for yourself so that you can have a deeper relationship with them and their entire network. Take time to read what they are posting. Understand why it is important to them and engage in a conversation from that perspective. That will build a deeper connection, rapport, and trust, and increase the relationship at a record pace.

   I recently did this with some powerful Blockchain connections in Europe. I was asked to sit in on some meetings related to Cryptocurrency and Blockchain, which I knew little about. I went to my current network on LinkedIn, typed in the related keywords, found first-level connections, called the ones I knew, and asked, "Who should I know?" They gave me some global connections even *they* did not know well.

   Next, I went to their profiles, and learned more about who they were and their respective missions based on their social media posts and articles they had written. I then engaged with them on some of their posts and commented on an article or two they wrote. Then I sent a direct message to each new connection on LinkedIn and sharing that I liked their work and would love to connect. Within five days, five of the people I reached out to responded. As a result I had three meetings. Two of them asked me for a Skype call before I even had the chance to ask them!

See how easy connecting can be online if you just have an understanding of *who* to reach out to and then *how* to best connect with them? The underlying reality with building online digital influence is that people want to be affirmed for their thought leadership and professionalism and that when you take the time to connect with them thoughtfully, you will get better results more often.

Power Move: *Reach out to Three People on Your Team.*

Find three people from your team who you care about and want to have a deeper business relationship with. Go and find their content online, seek to figure out what matters to them currently, and engage with them through their social media posts at a deeper level. Make it all about them!

FIRST Thought Leadership Share

The essence of your *first* thought-leadership share is that you're taking content that is from somebody at your level of influence in your industry or higher. These are people you admire, and with whom you want to connect. Maybe you're in relationship with them, or maybe you're not. The main thing is that you're seeking other people who have a good number of followers.

They also have a level of thought leadership that you are hungry for. These are thought leaders whose success you'd like to replicate in your own unique way.

We call this "connecting the networks together." You take somebody else's content and share it. You're engaging at a much higher level by sharing it with your entire network.

Numbers always vary depending on the network and connections. But remember, your most effective social reach, by definition, is within two degrees. That entails the people you're connected to, and those connected to your people. There is extreme power in this.

For example, if you had around 350 connections on LinkedIn, you could have a social reach by three degrees of over six million people. That's quite a few people, if you think about it. You have a powerful social reach. Whether they're all good connections or bad ones depends on how targeted your network is and then *how* you connect with them. Even if you have thousands of connections, the goal is to have deeper connections.

When you start sharing thought leadership articles from those you admire, they see that you have a targeted network, just like they do. You're sharing their thought leadership articles with your network for them. That creates a huge emotional connection while also creating value for them. Just as we talked about the power of that first engagement, imagine the power you have by sharing other thought leaders' content with your network.

The good news is that these thought leaders will see your sharing. When you do this, make sure that you provide some thought leadership commentary in addition to sharing their content. Remember, with every post you're making, you're starting a conversation.

You're taking someone else's thought-leadership article, tagging them in it, and adding your own thoughtful *Comment*. You're attaching your voice to the article within LinkedIn, Facebook, and Twitter. You'll see that @ sign and type their name. Make sure that it looks them up and that the link is viable. You're essentially leveraging your influence by connecting these influencers to your network and also getting yourself connected into their network.

Instantaneously, you get extreme visibility. Your new thought leader connections see how you are affirming them. They are now connected to you. Many times, this is an effective approach to becoming connected and generating relationships with these thought leaders. They will truly appreciate you doing this.

Don't Forget the Local Guys

Be sure you're paying attention to your local influencers, too. When you engage locally, it creates a rich groundswell of potential. These are folks who are up-and-comers. They're on the rise in business right in your neck of the woods.

You might want to create a list called "People to Watch in _____ (Fill in the blank with the year)." Keep building and posting about them throughout the year. Two or three months later, you could do an update, a "Where are They Now?" Show how they keep growing. Remember to keep this aligned with your goals and target connections. You're building your ideal network continuously.

Power Move: *Share content at your level of influence or higher.*

Make a list of the top 5 thought leaders in your industry with whom you would like to build relationships. Next, start engaging with them by sharing their content. On the surface, when you first begin doing this, you may get a little twinge that feels like they're your competitors. But those people are already successful and they don't see you as a competitor. They see you as an ally. Your goal is therefore to build relationships with them by connecting with them and their content, and then sharing it with your network.

Know the "Feeling" of Your *FIRST* Conversion

Your *first* conversion will happen when you share content from someone you might think is an impossible thought leader for you to connect to -- perhaps along the lines of Bill Gates, Oprah Winfrey, or Richard Branson. Go ahead and dare to think about people who feel like they're completely out of reach.

In my own thought leadership share, I tested this by connecting and engaging online with folks on this level. Don't expect immediate results. After a period of time and a little bit of effort—depending on how far removed they are—then BAM! You get a response back and begin establishing a connection with them. You get a high level of conversion.

In practical terms, the reality is that your first conversions may come from people who are more local -- those who haven't reached that upper echelon (elite, elite, elite). Maybe you think of it as billionaire status, or however you judge that.

The main point here is to keep going for the first next-best conversion. It's important to be conscious of how you feel about that first conversion. When somebody whose content you're sharing reaches out, acknowledges you, and makes the connection, reach back out and try to set up a face-to-face meeting if at all possible.

If they're too distant or too busy, schedule some sort of a meeting where you can see each other on camera via Skype or Zoom. Your goal is to create a deeper level of conversation with them. This starts when you see each other's faces. This is the basis for developing your *first* conversion. It's important for everyone to stay with those feelings and enjoy how good that feels. It is achievable with each and every person.

Power Move: *Write out your experience.*

Write a short note to yourself about how your *first* conversion made you feel. Whether it was a meeting, interview, referral or even a new deal. List how you felt about it—how good you felt, how affirmed — whatever's coming up for you. Know that you're creating a whole new level of consciousness with them.

Once you start grounding yourself, feeling happy with your results, you'll be hungry to create more of the same. Each future conversion you achieve will become smoother and even more fulfilling.

FIRST Conversation Starters: Posting With Purpose, 3-2-1

The idea of having a conversation on social media is no different than having one in person. As I shared previously, view connecting online through social media as a large networking event. It's just another forum where people are looking to make good connections and start interesting, beneficial conversations. The idea is that whenever you're going to post, share, or *Comment* on something, be conversational.

Many times, people make the mistake of believing that social media is solely a place for announcements. But it's far better to establish yourself and someone who is good at starting unique, engaging, value-added conversations first.

For instance, you wouldn't walk into a networking event where you say something like: "I want you to attend my next webinar. It's amazing! You're all going to enjoy it. It's on personal branding. Please go to my website to register. See you later! Bye," and then exit the room.

Many times, people new to social media (if they've only seen it used as an announcement platform) fall into the trap of just sticking with the above example. This is why sometimes people hesitate to post because it can feel too salesy or gimmicky. Instead, as I said above, start a conversation by acknowledging the insights of others with whom you want to connect, first. Seek to come across as a thought leader. Whatever you're sharing, be clear that you have important things to say and make yourself approachable.

There's a viable methodology to this. In my company, we've always maintained the following principle: whether we're doing this for a client or we're teaching it, the key is to make a 5:1 ratio on posts. This involves you first creating five genuinely good conversational posts. Once you've done that, you can make a *Call to Action*. In essence, by first giving support to others you have created enough goodwill to make a request for yourself (aka your *Call to Action*).

Your *Call to Action* involves making an announcement without a need to create a conversation. If you're new at this, you want to warm up your audience for at least a month of rotations. This would involve you making about five or six posts a week for about four weeks. Then post your first Call to Action.

However, if you post a Call to Action before you start a number of robust conversations, it won't endear you to anyone. Few will truly care about what you're offering. I never recommend taking that tack. When you're doing that online, the language is a little bit different.

Another tip here is that whenever you do make a Call to Action post that is meant to drive somebody to download something or go to your event, webinar, webcast, or white paper (whatever that looks like) *invite them*. Ask them to join you. This way, your post will feel more like a welcoming conversation or invitation as opposed to an announcement.

3-2-1

This roadmap for posting success involves a rotation of six that's broken down as 3-2-1. The 3-2-1 methodology is as follows:

- 3: Create 3 thought leadership educational and inspirational conversation starters.
- 2: Add 2 personal posts mixed in with those.
- 1: Offer 1 call to action, that again, isn't a demand or command. I's an invitation.

Breaking it down further:

3 - Three thought leadership educational and inspirational conversation starters

These could be articles that you, a colleague, or team member has written. By sharing someone else's article, you're again working toward relationship building. It's key to be sure that whatever your threes in this 3-2-1 recipe are, they consist of thought leadership.

These could be original content or content contributed by others. However, don't only use other people's content. You want to develop your own voice and your own content. This means sharing an article you've written, a post, video, podcast, or infographic—something that you or your company has created. By posting these, you're starting a dialogue. So make sure these are conversational.

2 - Two personal posts (to a total of 6)

This helps you be seen as approachable and interesting, and it humanizes you to your followers.

For example, I was helping a client recently who was trying to decide which two personality posts he should include. Again, these posts are more about the individual thought leader as a person rather than about his or her business or career. My client happens to be a scratch golfer, so he said, "Well, maybe I should just give golf tips. I love to give people golf tips."

He has a ton of these, so that piqued my interest. I replied, "I would love to see your golf tips because I'm far from being a scratch golfer, just like most other folks. I would actually check into that and hear what you have to say, not only because of your expertise, but because I trust you, too."

Other things that fit into this personality category could be as simple as you sharing something about your favorite sport or team. It might be a restaurant that you've tried, and you're giving them a good shout-out. (Yes, this is even okay to do once in a while on LinkedIn.) Don't necessarily share constant foodie shots of what you had for lunch, etc. That's more for Instagram.

In terms of being a business influencer, we're interested in who you are and what you do. Perhaps there are charitable organizations that you work with that you'd like to mention and feature. While we were going through and building your story during the initial intake process, we found and discovered things that other people (peers) will find interesting about you. Those are the kinds of things to include in your two personal posts.

1 - One Call to Action that's a friendly invitation for someone to feel like they're joining you on something or following you to get something of extremely high value.

Educational materials are excellent for this. Not only are those a learning point, they're a big trust-building point. I'll give you a quick example that we might typically use with our Social Jack offerings. You can use that as a template to tweak, create your own unique verbiage, and make it your own.

EX: "We would love it if you could join us at our next Master Class/ webinar/broadcast. In appreciation, we're going to give each and every one of you a copy of our new e-book."

Notice how that felt different than "Attend our next event—It's going to be amazing. We're going to teach you X Y Z." That sort of carnival barker approach is more about me and my organization than it is about you. In marketing, we talk about WIIFM (What's in it for me?) We always say if you're speaking on behalf of the customer, that's great. It's not about you, the marketer, or person doing the Call to Action. It's about them.

Think about your ideal target. What's important to them? Speak to them through your writing as if you're standing before them and inviting them to your next event.

Again, all of these should be conversational. If you stick by this rule, we can guarantee that you'll experience far greater engagement and success.

Power Move: *Anticipate and participate in a two-way conversation.*

As you practice the above Move, remember again to watch for responses. Make sure that you are expecting people to talk or write back and create two-way conversation. Anticipate that, and therefore, even when people send back a simple, "Thank you, I'll check it out," continue a conversation with them. Have another volley and say, " Terrific! Let me know if you have any questions." That's all you have to say.

It doesn't have to be long. You can do it on your mobile application. You have set it up to receive notifications when people respond to you on any of these postings, so make sure that you're there for the other side of the conversation. By doing so, you ensure that you're building rapport and relationship the entire time.

Get Your *FIRST* Referrals

The final piece of this is knowing that when you're engaging with the thought leaders and your team, it's time to start looking at who's in their network. Who, within that network, do you desire to connect with next? We want you to be conscious of the fact that most people you're connecting to are well connected. It's not too hard in today's world with social media. Once you're connected to somebody and engaging with them, you must be aware of who else is doing the same.

It's no different than being at a live event and standing in a circle of people. Maybe you know five of those people, and there are three more you don't know. But here you are in this conversation. As it progresses, you discover you want to get to know those people more. You might even want to have them on your team.

This is how you grow your influence and increase the influence that others can then have through you. It's about *asking* for introductions, referrals, meetings, connections, and thus relationships—outcomes that are directly connected to your goals. Also remember to connect with them on social media. This is a tactical Power Move to connect your two networks.

Bring this practice to a much higher level by engaging with thought leaders. Begin the process of getting your first referrals by taking time to know *who* your connections know. Also work on offering your first referrals to those people. Many times when I'm doing this, I offer referrals first.

As that relationship starts to flourish, you have the opportunity to ask for a referral to someone you know is in their network. You can also keep offering referrals to that other person. What's cool about this is when you start engaging with other thought leaders, with your team and network at this higher level, your network will begin to work for you. Instead of always having to ask for referrals, you'll have the enjoyment of waking up and seeing referrals appear in your inbox.

Your goal here is to pursue making requests for referrals. Note that there's a tipping point where you start generating referrals that are unsolicited. You are present and building rapport with your network. This should be your goal with a vision of making this process a normal part of your daily work life. As you become adept at practicing these higher levels of engagement, you naturally attract new people and new opportunities to you.

A magical aspect of this process is that you will start getting referrals from the connections from those on your team and the people they know, so on and so on.

This is part of the three degrees of separation in your network I mentioned earlier. With this, you won't be getting referrals directly through that person. People in their network will find you and come to you on their own.

That's the most interesting thing about practicing this process. When you're more active in your network, you're *seen* as an active participant in the network. In response, the network becomes more active with you, and those referrals keep coming. That's the magic.

> **Note:** *When someone is giving you a referral, do not jump ahead eight steps and connect to all their social media channels and start engaging and messaging them. That is way out of rapport. Wait for the introduction from your connected party and explore their social media profile for research. Then ask to connect on LinkedIn. Follow them on Twitter or other follow-type business channels.*

Remember, Facebook and some other channels may be very private for people. Wait until you get a little further into the relationship and proceed slowly as you get to know more about the person. I typically wait for people to connect with me on Facebook even though I'm an open networker there. If you're not sure, ask them where they'd like to connect with business relationships. They will tell you.

Power Move: *Provide referrals.*

Remember to provide referrals to those with whom you're at a Level 3 or below—provide and give referrals. Before you ask others for referrals, make sure you're at a Level 3 or above with them. Simply look at their network and ask for the people you want as referrals. It's that straightforward.

YOUR *FIRST*
Real Community

FIRST Connection to Network Science (Clusters and Hubs)

As we embark on understanding our relationship with the individuals we're targeting in our network, we will begin to form clusters and hubs around us, which will then become a community. People will become tuned into you as a brand. They'll be tuned into your business and your company. This is humanizing the brand within an organization. We start with people first, and then connect them and their networks. This makes an accelerating brand.

This was part of the conundrum with employee advocacy. Companies, through no fault of their own (an evolution step), were conveying, "Well, here's a controlled platform. We're going to give you all the ability to share this amazing content on behalf of the brand." By doing that, most companies left the individuals out.

It's still that way today and will be tomorrow because people believe, "Oh, it's so great to have this group or this team of employees sharing our content." It shows that they're champions of the brand.

However, they left the people out, which is why you start with the professional, the individual. There's a natural attraction to that, which therefore attracts people to the brand. You can still function as a team around the brand, but it is with the voice of each individual. They need to be trained on this to truly be amazing brand ambassadors!

As a business influencer in today's online-centric world, you should be focused on building your own community (online and offline), facing in and facing outside of your organization. Your plan should be to build a better, higher-level community. As you are constantly connecting, engaging, and sharing yourself—your thought leadership blended with compassion and caring—people will be attracted to you. As you consistently tend to your connections, you will gain a following.

On Twitter, your connections are called followers, right? You also get followed on Facebook and LinkedIn. Your followers will stay tuned in to you, just like a brand (like a TV station). This is your first real community. In this chapter, we start with your first connection to network science.

I like network science because it shows us how we are connected. Here we are referred to as nodes; however, I prefer to say individual because every one of us is not like the other. We're unique, which is what makes us individuals. The minute we connect to somebody, that's a connection. LinkedIn even calls them "connections."

As we make this connection and begin to create the early parts of our network formation, we begin to play in a targeted environment where we attract and gain relationships with like-minded people. We begin to form what is termed "clusters."

And then, at some point, as we begin to grow further connections, we create a "hub" of connections. Here, people are attracted to the hubs we have created and, as a result, they want to connect to us. From there, our networks not only grow in size but in quality, which is even more important. In other words, stronger relationships equal stronger connections.

Secondly, there is a connection between two targeted nodes. When you think of "targeted nodes" with social team building, it's crucial to remember "target."

The third component of network science consists of clusters. A cluster is made up of several linked nodes. People who are like-minded. In the business sense, let's say you're looking for executive V.P.s in manufacturing. You connect two of those and that becomes a link. They start to form several linked nodes, which then blossom into a cluster. You then have a cluster of manufacturing V.P.s and people related to them.

The fourth component is a hub or a large cluster, possibly several related clusters formed together. Again, thinking of that target, this could be within an organization like a Fortune 500 company such as GE, Microsoft, or Google. In actuality, those are big hubs, even though they're companies.

Dissecting this down even more, within them, they have hubs based on divisions, departments, industries, etc. This is how I want you to think when it comes to forming social teams. Network science is a template we can structure ourselves moving toward that ideal target or that ideal championship. Now you can see where there is some crossover/overlap between sports and military science.")

Don't connect just for the sake of connecting. Connect to organizations and groups that make sense and complement your areas of expertise and interest. Look for the people in those hubs who can build the best relationship with you. This is important to successful social teaming.

Power Move: *Notice what is working and leverage that.*

When you go online, realize that you are now becoming a hub. So take the time to look around and see who's tuning in to you, who you're attracting, and whether they're the right people. In other words, do they match your target? It's that simple.

In fact, LinkedIn now has special tools that will report: "You have these types of people looking at your profile"—such as "CEOs and salespeople are viewing your profile." If those are not the right people, you're not having the right conversations or right engagements with those targets. If you find that is the case, go back and reread the earlier chapters that address goals and targets.

It's the concept that you can create hubs and be one of the leaders in that hub. Earlier, I gave the example of Billy, who formed a committee in an executive organization to which he belonged, to help people of color get on to corporate boards. Billy had basically set up a hub of connection. As a result, when companies are looking for diverse candidates, Billy is someone they contact to help them. Once you create a hub, it's like a boomerang. Here, the benefits come back to you on a continuous basis.

Power Move: *Explore building a hub within your current network.*

Look at the organizations where you currently network and ask yourself, "Where could I build a hub that I could lead?" Also ask, "Where can I add the most value? Where are the places I can add it?" Write down the answers that come to you and then take action.

Remember: the ongoing sustainability of your network is about you building robust hubs of connection.

You Can Start from Scratch. If I Did It, So Can You.

Flashback: As I mentioned earlier, after I was let go from Merrill Lynch, I took a low-paying data entry job to survive. I was twenty-one years old and needed to get a leg up. A wonderful programmer, along with some inside knowledge provided by her husband, helped me do just that by connecting me with Midland-Ross in Cicero. I got hired to write programming for them at a much higher pay scale. It was a turning point that enabled me to start moving up the corporate ladder financially and got me thinking outside the box in a big way.

My entrepreneurial roots then rose to the challenge, and I opened my first company, right at that moment. I began networking with some of my instructors and fellow graduates from school. We opened an office on Wacker Drive within 90 days. During that startup time, I was working on that payroll system so that I had a steady, decent income once more.

As my company brought in new work, I got my pay up to the neighborhood of $1,500 a week. From that point on, I just kept increasing my rate. Clients kept rolling in, and the new network was building. One relationship bridged me to another. From this network I then started getting steady referrals that turned into new job opportunities.

I had chosen one of my former instructors to be my business partner. Before long, I discovered he was into cocaine. Money went strangely missing out of the business account. I was in another bad business situation with a cokehead who was embezzling from me.

My first thought was "Are you kidding me?!?" followed shortly by "I'm going to figure a way out of this ASAP. I'm not letting another drug addict ruin all my hard work." I'd been working my ass off programming, networking, and building up all of these accounts. At this point, he didn't realize that I knew what he'd been up to. One day he told me, "Hey, I think we ought to put everything in your name because I'm going through this divorce."

I spoke to an attorney and disclosed to him what was going on. He advised me to make the move as fast as I could because it would put me in control. This made my escape plan from my partner that much easier. So I told him, "You know what? That's a great idea." As soon as we completed all the paperwork putting the business solely in my name, I wrote him a check for half of everything in the bank account and told him he was fired. That was my first hostile takeover, and I was only twenty-three.

It's All About Your Connections

I continued networking and doing business from that moment forward. This was a period of my life where I met other hard-working professionals who became and still are some of my best trusted friends. But I soon realized that even though I had my programmer's certification, I was still non-degreed.

I didn't have significant experience in business yet. Some pieces were missing from my knowledge base, such as accounting and a few other areas. Even though I was learning a lot by writing a payroll system, I was still wanting in certain components on the business side of the world.

I networked my way into a CPA firm that allowed me to help open their first management advisory services department. I helped lead MAS for a CPA firm—all without a degree. I enrolled at DePaul to continue my education. My network was building in a new direction with the accounting firm employees, clients, and others along the way.

I was blending networks, taking two clusters and bringing them together to form a larger network—a bigger team around me. It was so easy to develop and find clients that way. I used my network whenever I needed to find something or get something, whether it was personal or in business. Someone in that network always proved to be connected. It was present and working all around me.

When you build a network of relationships as opposed to just one-off deals, you'll never regret it. That time in my life was my big epiphany. I had finally discovered how to belong, not just keep connecting in order to get the next piece. Many of my friends who went through some extremely dire times with me are still with me today. In the words of the long-running Mastercard slogan, "That's priceless."

Your *FIRST* Responsibilities

It's time to determine your first responsibilities. You must realize that you are a community manager *for you*. You are now responsible for maintaining your level of thought leadership. That's why you use the system of working 20 minutes a day in social media. Working in a routine where you're not spending all your time there, rather you're connecting in person with people, the right people (your social team).

However, when you are online, you're a community manager. You are that business influencer (thought leader), the person people are attracted to. You are the person that people want to connect with, attach to, be with. In doing that, you have a responsibility to make sure that you're serving those people and that you're feeling the attention and nourishment it affords, not the stress from it.

Make sure you enjoy that part of the responsibility. It's a "want to" not a "have to." Have fun with it. Remember, you're connecting, getting affirmed, feeling good with others feeling good about being with you! Sometimes, this is where you engage your social team even more to help you along the way, to share those responsibilities. This can take place through content, engagement, or through having them work with you, to help you, support you, or step in for you.

There's something called an "Influencer Takeover." You reach out and ask, "Hey, could you jump in and help take over my channel or my network for a week? I'm going to be out. I would love you to tend to my community for me." It's important that you understand that it's okay to play together. It's okay to ask for help along the way. As a thought leader, you get to coach and train them on what that looks like and how they can do that for themselves, too!

Power Move: *Recognize and develop your community manager role.*

Make sure that you realize that you're a community manager. See yourself in that role. Be sure you ask for help from your social team when it comes to managing your community.

FIRST Team Support

This leads into your *first* team support. Remember when we got into social teaming and set the responsibility of us asking for referrals, asking for better connections, networking up? We were working with our team to do this, engaging with our team. We're now becoming more of a hub, so make sure that you don't forget to go to your team.

This is a perfect time to look at your social team and ask, "Is this the right team?" You'll recall in social teaming that you're constantly scouting and drafting every day. Don't get too comfortable with the team, or you're going to be comfortable where you are. You're not going to reach your goals and objectives.

Your first team support is super important. It's about going to your team, asking them to help you in the responsibilities of community management, and seeing who rises to the occasion. They may do this by providing thought leadership articles and comments, or they may help you talk with the people in your network. Earlier in the book, I equated social media as being like a live, networking event.

We had a great event in Chicago called BARE Networking. My friend and CEO of Networlding Publishing book creation firm, Melissa G. Wilson, helped out with this. We held the number of participants to very few people to to ensure the best success. I reached out to a few folks in my network and said, "Okay, each of us invites 10 people to this event with a goal of getting 30-40 high level people together." Three of us went into our networks and invited 10 people each.

Within eight days, we had sixty people and a waiting list. That was how I empowered my team to support me in that live event. We did no email, social media, or advertising promotion. In fact, the event was private. We simply each invited high-level connections we knew were good networkers.

You're doing the exact same thing on social media. Your first realization of team support is that you not only have a team but that you are going to utilize them. Either don't have the right relationship with that team or don't have the right team."

Power Move: *Ask for support.*

Go to your team and ask for ongoing team support. Be aware of who steps up and who doesn't respond.

FIRST Feel The Love

First feel of the love is always important to me. As a child, I had early abandonment issues. Those don't just stay stuck in the past, in your early development. Neuroscience research has shown that's part of how we're formed, and how we are wired as human beings, which means that we need this attachment. It's a core human need to be connected, to feel love. This is where I want you to get into the emotions of being a community manager. Really embrace and love the feeling.

I guarantee you that fears will come up around this, and they'll try to snuff out the love. Fears that I discussed earlier in the book will come up, such as not having enough time, or that you don't matter, or that people are absolutely unwilling to help you.

The thing to bear in mind is everyone is busy. They have lives, "stuff," and all kinds of challenges show up in everyone's narrative. If they're not stepping up for you in the way that you expect or need, please remember that it may not be personal at all. It just may not be the appropriate time for them to be on your team.

Now it's time to make sure that you feel the relationship, the love of the people helping you. Make sure you don't forget to thank them, both personally and on social media. This will take you to a whole new level of building rapport with your community.

The minute you can feel the love and gratitude of the people you're serving in your community, it's nothing short of exquisite. You need to just slow down, pause, and take that in. This will be the day when this entire part of social media and digital-business influence becomes the turning point for you.

The key here is continuously practicing the *art* and *science* of creating mutually beneficial (rather than haphazard) relationships in your network. This goes back to Billy Dexter's book, *Making Your Net Work*.

Additionally, if you want to take it a step further, Dexter emphasizes that creating mutually beneficial relationships is strategic and takes practice, but is essential to sustained success in networking.

Power Move: *Thank all those contributing to your success, regularly.*

Take a moment to think of those people who are helping you as part of your social team. Then look at those in your community who are responding to you. Pause for a moment and just soak in the love.

Don't forget to thank them on social media with a note: "Thank you for your response. I appreciate your comments." Make sure that for the ones who are stepping up you do a "Gratitude Post: "Thank you for all your support this week in helping me to grow and develop my business influence." Don't forget to thank those people along the way. It's okay to do it publicly. If you're not comfortable doing this, do it privately via a phone call, text, or email.

Make sure you're in the practice of giving that gratitude and love back to others. Pause and allow the reflection of that love and gratitude to soak into you as well. By doing this, you will start to understand what the others in your network experience by being on the receiving end of feeling the love. You'll be reminded that you, along with all of those in your network, deserve to feel reciprocity with love and gratitude as you all create a beautiful balance of giving and receiving.

MEASURING YOUR
First Levels of
Success

A common phrase typically used in sales is applicable here: "Don't mistake activities for results." It's also just a good rule of thumb for life in general. Do your best to not get caught up in all of the activity you're generating without tying what you are doing to the results you want to achieve.

This is a reminder to be conscious of the goals and objectives that I suggested you set up at the beginning of this book. If you haven't set those goals and objectives up yet, do so now. You can't improve what you can't measure. Make sure that whether you're building your social networking team or generating content and engagement online, you stay focused on moving towards the goals you desire to achieve.

Take time as you're measuring your first levels of success to tune into what your results might look like and how it will feel. Once again, move more into the emotional side of your vision. It's important that you get emotionally connected to your own success.

As you go through your Power Moves, reaching out and connecting through your networking partners, you'll soon realize that your outreach has resulted in an appointment or an interview, a meeting of some sort. Whether you're sales-minded, career-minded, or overall success-minded, keep track of these first level successes. These opportunities are the foundation for building sales and/or your career, and at the same time, they build your brand.

So what are some of the first signs of success? If people are responding to you even in a simple conversation, that's a good first sign of success. This response could be in the form of a phone call or an agreement to set a face-to-face meeting.

It's the same thing in the digital world. As you begin to see people appear in your newsfeed, you will become aware of who they are, and in this world of social, you will also see through their posts what matters to them. From that vantage point, you can see the services or products (for sales opportunities) or skills (for career opportunities) you have to offer that could be of value to them. As you engage with them, offering your support and insights that address their needs, you are advancing up the first success level as you build out your network.

As you continue to engage and *show* people your value through the insights you share online, you will begin to see other people responding to you. This is a phenomenal validation of success. As the saying goes, "Birds of a feather flock together." Your span of influence will expand to others with similar values, connections that your current network holds. As you *purposely and purposefully* post, you will build your *social proof*,which is all about growing your influence.

As a result of nurturing your network online, you will see *their network* start to reach out to you. And the best news is that you won't have to initiate the conversation first. That's beautiful. These connections of your connections will start coming to you. This is termed "inbound marketing." I consider this outreach the ultimate first sign of success.

That's what people don't realize about LinkedIn. It is the ultimate connection machine. Here, your efforts at steadily nurturing your network through value-added posting and commenting will create the kind of credibility that puts you first in your network and your network's network.

Power Move: *Document your success.*

As you see these signs of success, write them down. Journal them. In fact, keep a separate journal for these successes. This way whenever you feel what you are doing is not paying off, you can go back to that journal. You will see that all the value you planted out into your network is germinating and has started bearing fruit. Keep returning to this journal and anchor yourself in the validation that you are adding value to the lives of others, value that will pay off again and again.

Remember, if any fears arise, just "name them to tame them." Write them down and then look at what they really mean. What do they show you? Recognize that you have taken the time to offer and create value for your network. As such, you will see the return on your efforts. Realize that often success can breed fear. If you have too many people responding to you, you might have the fear of being overwhelmed.

As I mentioned before, you may think something like, "Oh, but I won't have enough time to respond and deliver on all of these responses. Now others might see me as someone who is not genuine." Face your fears so that you don't shut down. The last thing you want is to step out of the *first* system and give up on the process that was your roadmap to building vibrant networks of support on sustainable value.

Get Known as *FIRST*

Of course, you want to be known as *first* in your network. But when somebody else shows up out of the blue and says, "I'm starting a new project, and I thought of you first," that's a whole new ballgame. It's a big deal. I believe it's important for us to understand it, feel it, and acknowledge it, as well as help instill it in others.

I received a call recently from a global initiative, somebody with a far bigger budget on a marketing project than I had when I was building call centers and doing some work with Sears and other Fortune 500 companies. This call came from the founder and CEO of an entrepreneurial company I've known for over ten years.

He started the conversation by stating, "I'm getting funded, and the dollar amount is north of $200 million. I have a $20 million budget for marketing, and I thought of you first." To be completely honest, a lot of fear came up with that call.

My first panicky reaction was *Oh, no! How am I going to do that? Am I going to be good enough? Why is he calling on me?* But then, remembering my own advice to others, I took a deep breath and got it together enough to change my inner dialogue.

It became: *Wait a minute. This is a game changer. This could change our entire company. It could help us grow without needing to continue seeking outside capital like we're currently doing. Okay, so let's have a conversation and see what's really going on.*

Rather than worry about the fear, I chose to switch the conversation to building rapport and listening deeply to understand the needs of my colleague. I focused on connecting with him and learning as much as I could.

That approach felt so much better. Every time a question came up, I began seeking an answer from him so that I could clarify and understand exactly what the project could look like and what the growth of his company could look like (what they really needed).

Once I took the dollars out of the picture, I was able to focus on just listening and understanding their needs.

Once we finished talking, I thanked him for thinking of me *first*. It felt extremely gratifying. So the lesson here is that when you're presented with the initial signs of success, acknowledge that you were thought of *first*. Next, take a deep breath, and then listen. Ask clarifying questions. This is always a good time to review your goals. You'll start to realize, "Oh, my gosh, I'm getting found *first*. I'm getting known *first* in my network for what I love to do. Now I can achieve my goals with my ideal targets."

You're training and wiring your brain to be more conscious of the fact that every move you make drives you toward that point of being known *first*. That's a big deal in anyone's network or industry. Once that occurs, you become that go-to person. As a result, people in your network will say things like: "Oh, you need to talk to X (You)" or "You need to meet with X (You) or "You need X (You)!"

This started happening for me four or five years ago. I had some pivotal shifts before I was known in telecommunications, then in enterprise resource planning (ERP). I also became known *first* for quite a long while in the field of customer relationship management (CRM).

As I evolved in my career and started to focus and build my social media skills, I started to become an expert on LinkedIn. As a result, I was able to start building my career as a digital business influence expert before the term became popular.

Analyze Your *FIRST* Metrics

Now is the time to ask, "What do the metrics look like when it comes to measuring success?" As I shared earlier, on LinkedIn and other platforms, you can see who's viewing your profile; in other words, who's looking at you. When you view who's looking at you, ask yourself whether these people are your ideal targets.

This is a good exercise for metrics analysis. If you are not being viewed by people with whom you want to network, then you will need to revise your profile and keyword optimize it to attract more targeted connections.

Engagement

This might be a good time to revisit previous sections of this book regarding engagement. Engagement, for our purposes, involves starting value-added conversations on social media. Target those people who would be good network partners. Create a goal to reach out to five people each day, those who would be ideal networking partners. From there, set a goal for your numbers to go up.

Appointments/Calls

Let's say you're a CEO, and you want to get your company funded, or buy another company. You have certain types of capital connections that you want to make as part of achieving that outcome. On the other hand, if you're seeking career advancement, search for active people on LinkedIn who are in your targeted companies, and then reach out through your current network to get introduced to those people to set up interviews.

Either way, be sure to set goals to reach out as often as possible, and then set goals to track your success. Melissa G. Wilson, top networking expert, says that today, "The introduction is the new referral." In other words, because social media sites, especially those that are dedicated to building professional networks (like LinkedIn), offer a platform for both *showcasing* and *leveraging* your influence. Here, your profile becomes your launch pad for achieving major success as you request regular introductions.

With her social science background, Melissa refers to this as the "Transference of Trust." Here, she adds that when you use this introduction request process, you set the social table to continuously leverage your connections to collapse either sales or career cycles by upwards of 50 percent or more. As a result, you *accelerate* goal achievement like never before.

With either of the above examples, you might work to set up multiple phone and/or in-person appointments or interviews. Be sure you set reasonable goals so you don't become overwhelmed. You may be perfectly happy with three appointments a week, or with three appointments a day. It's up to you and your comfort level. I work with some people who want five appointments a day. It all depends upon whether these are phone, Skype, or in-person appointments.

When making online appointments, find some way to see your connection on the screen, at least for your first meeting. There are many platforms from which to choose. Of course, a face-to-face meeting is an excellent way to build connection and rapport. Your goal is to score the number of appointments and calls that you want each week.

Sales/Job Offers

Last but far from least, if you're in sales, make sure you're tracking how your efforts are generating those sales. If you're looking for job offers, interviews would be classified as appointments. Again, whether looking inside or outside your organization, if you're looking for bigger things (business owners, executives looking for things organizationally), those results could look like transactions or contracts of different sorts.

As long as you're tracking your efforts and celebrating the milestones along the way, you'll be successful with your efforts.

Power Move: *Find an accountability partner.*

Establish what you're tracking, your minimum starting point. It's okay to have a floor and a ceiling here, but also get a peer review partner or coach (your accountability partner) engaged with this part of the conversation. This is where the rubber hits the road and you generate success.

Score Your Real First Return on Investment (ROI)

Up to this point, I haven't told you to spend a lot of money. But we're talking about you utilizing your time differently so that you can be known in your network as that first go-to person. Your time is worth money, right? Put a value on your time. Is your time worth $100 an hour, $200 an hour? You can calculate this based on a number of things if you don't have a cut-and-dried answer right off the bat.

You have a billable rate, or you make a certain amount of money within a year. As you're calculating ROI, maybe you have a coach, or plan to hire one. Think about buying some tools, additional education to help support you on this, more training sessions. Whatever that looks like, continue to invest in yourself.

As you make those investments, track that in the period of time when you're getting these results. That way, you know if (for example) you're spending $400 of your time per week and generating $2,000 in sales, you have a return on investment. You know exactly how much money you're making, how much the effort is paying off, and you're conscious of the financial side of this.

You can make determinations as to how you expand this throughout your team. You might reach the point where you're like, "Holy smokes! I can hire a personal assistant to help me and move to that next level of return on investment for myself." Without diving too deeply into the math of all this, I do want to make sure that you are conscious of it.

Power Move: *Evaluate your time value and ROI.*

Understand the value of your time. Do some simple scoring of the appointments, calls, sales, or job offers that you're getting. These are a good ROI. If not, ask yourself and your coach (or accountability partner) some questions about why that is. You may need:

- better appointments.
- a clearer message.
- better conversations to attract better people.
- to ask your Social Team for " HELP!"
- to go back and read through previous chapters of this book and work a little slower on some of the areas. It's always a good rule of thumb to have a periodic mini-refresher course.

Feel Your *FIRST* Personal Power

It's time to luxuriate in the results of your efforts. Revel in the enjoyment of knowing that you don't have to spend a lot of time to generate a lot of success. This is why I want you to maintain those 20 minutes a day on social media. I want you to understand that in small increments, by using a lot of Power Moves that are either one, three, or five minute exercises, you can be golden and absolutely enjoy your freedom and personal power.

Those three-to-five minute increments carved out of your 20 minutes a day (spent in a focused manner) can absolutely generate and build relationships, not only with individuals but also with entire networks, clusters, and hubs. In doing this, you'll recognize that all this power is within you.

You don't have to buy special tools. You can use those types of things to supplement. The power you need to build that ideal social team—that network, that case for you being known within the network—is all within you. That is extremely empowering. Don't just feel your freedom; feel your personal power in this.

FIRST
Celebration

FIRST Gather Your Team

In prior chapters, I've indicated that your success is dependent on you *feeling* your success. I want you not only to feel the love, but also to feel the gratitude of others. Feel your social team embracing and supporting you. All of this helps prevent you from feeling alone. In addition, please be sure that you celebrate your success.

Celebration is something that as an entrepreneur and hard-working business professional (all those striving to develop their influence) you need to remember to do. It's vitally important to celebrate your successes so that you keep building enthusiasm. From there, you can leverage your energy toward your next success and so on and so on.

To create a true celebration, invite your team to get together. They will enjoy meeting one another and expanding their networks. Some of your team may not show up. Note who is there, who is not, and who participates. Again, your goal is to achieve mutual success. Those who participate in exchanging support and opportunities are the loyal members of your team.

With today's virtual meetings technology, there should be no excuses from your team not to show, unless they are not ready to be on your team! Remember, it's all about the quality of your network, not about the numbers.

Power Move: *Organize your team and celebrate!*

Organize and gather your team, whether it's virtual, in person, or a combination, in order to hold your celebration.

Not long ago, I assembled an amazing team for a celebratory meeting. All these folks were in different states across the U.S., with one team member in Canada. We conducted a Zoom call where I snapped a picture of all of us because it was the largest number of people we had to date. I felt humbled by the sheer number of participants.

I had a grid of about fifteen people on my screen simultaneously. It reminded me of the old *Hollywood Squares* game show or the opening credits of the classic sitcom, *The Brady Bunch*. Okay, am I dating myself now? We even joked about it during the call. We were talking and celebrating our collaboration on a national movement and the purpose behind that.

It was a very cool moment to have that team feel together, to share the unity of being on the same page and sharing our mission together. This needs to be something that you have fun with.

The main point is to have a lot of fun and not get hung up on the technology or that one person can't make that date. Schedule a time that's far enough in advance that it makes sense for everybody possible to make it, so you all can connect.

Establish Your *FIRST* Cycle of Gratitude

The second part is to establish the *first* cycle of gratitude. You're both feeling and expressing gratitude. I've already talked about the cycle of gratitude and putting gratitude posts online, but there's something unique about sharing face-to-face with somebody. You give them a handshake or a hug, and look in their eyes as you tell them how much you appreciate their partnership and how much it means to you. In many cases, they'll reflect that same expression.

The magic occurs when your team begins to connect with each other. The gratitude passes from one person to the next and comes back to you. Everyone will feel the gratitude because they're all part of this fantastic team and network. They're playing full out.

By now, you're starting to get the gratitude and appreciation of someone who's connected to someone within your team. I'm talking about people who show up unsolicited to tell you how much they appreciate you and what you've done.

I was walking in my building recently. This young lady in a red coat was getting on the elevator as I was dashing up to make it in before the doors closed. She saw me hurrying and quickly hit the hold button to wait for me. As I stepped in she called my name. I looked up and smiled, saying, "Oh, hi. How you doing?" I honestly had no idea who she was, but could tell she was excited to see me.

As she kept holding the door open, I started to feel a bit uncomfortable. My interior, fear-based dialogue was, "Oh, my gosh, what's going on here? She's holding up all these other people and inconveniencing them. The alarm's going to sound in a minute." She said, "I just wanted to tell you, my boss shared with me what you taught him and how much it's important to connect. I want to tell you how much I appreciate what you're doing in the world, and to make sure you know that I intend to connect with you, too."

That was a true magic moment for me. I was humbled, and my eyes teared up. Appropriate or not, I gave her a business hug as I said, "I just want to thank you so much. Anything you need, just let me know." I felt that cycle of gratitude.

Based on how I'm wired, it's important for me to pause and acknowledge beautiful moments like this one. It helps me realize that It's okay for any of us to just exist and accept that gratitude when it comes. To honestly feel that you deserve praise and are okay taking it in, without feeling any guilt about needing to give something back in that moment.

I have to catch myself, because the first thing I want to do is deflect that and give it back. Make sure you take time to allow the cycle of gratitude to happen for you. Paying attention to it because that's where the real rewards come in. Celebrate those simple special moments in your life.

Power Move: *Again, constantly celebrate your successful moments.*

Be on the lookout for these wonderful moments of appreciation coming through your network to you. In addition to awareness, journal these experiences so that you can appreciate them in the future.

Attend Your *FIRST* Networking Event

It's always an interesting experience to stay highly aware when you're walking into someone else's network. You may find that your network may well be part of someone else's network. Now you're attending a networking event that presents another opportunity for celebration -- much like social media!

Depending on how you're wired, you may be saying, "Oh, I *have* to go to such and such networking event." I never enjoy hearing people say, "Dean said I should go to two networking events a week, but I just don't like doing that."

To avoid resistance about attending those events, I suggest that you initially go to events where you know other people. This way you'll automatically be in a better position where you're okay talking with people. This will help you break the ice. As you go to these events, you'll feel more comfortable with attending because you will have a good time there.

But also note that you don't have to go alone. Consider taking a friend (a wing woman or man) with you for support. This will help you increase your connections and develop those mutually beneficial exchanges that lead to future opportunities for all involved.

In other words, a little bit of effort to engage and meet new people at events really can pay off over and over again when you are looking for a new job or new business opportunities. I have seen this happen over and over So, even if you're shy, try to get out there and connect!

When you meet someone—anyone you feel is a high-caliber person you'd like to draft onto your team—make note of this fact on the back of their business card or in one of your electronic notes on your cell phone. Later, reach out and set up a convenient time to getting better acquainted. Seize these unique opportunities when you recognize them.

You will find folks you want to meet and you'll find yourself thinking, "Oh, wow! She's just like Becky, and she's in my Top 5" or "This person reminds me of one of my key team members. I can see connecting and developing a similar level of connection with him/her, too."

Don't forget to switch the conversations you have as soon as possible to ask, "Tell me about what's most exciting in your life right now?" I have found that this question, first of all, gets people talking about something positive which is always a great place to start. It is also a wonderful beginning of engagement that will build off of itself.

As the person shares their story, take the time to really listen. Be on the lookout to discover things you both have in common creating a more genuine connection. Right after I leave an event, I sit down and journal the celebration of meeting new people.

Celebrate the powerful feeling of making great connections by visualizing the potential of the various outcomes that those connections can have if you both move to a collaborative exchange of support and opportunity creation -- Scouting and Drafting. Sound familiar?

Whenever you go to a networking event, a meeting, or even when people show up at an informal gathering at a Starbucks, be sure you understand there's always potential to start building mutually beneficial networking opportunities. When you first meet potential key team members, take note of it and celebrate that you've met.

There's this moment of epiphany where you may realize that new person could potentially grow into one of the biggest game-changing relationships of your life. We have all this power within us. If we notice it and enjoy the moment, we know that meeting people can always be a celebration.

Power Move: *Celebrate your connections.*

Make sure as you're attending your *first* or next networking event after reading this book, you also celebrate each magical connection. Remember, this will not be everybody, just those people you can visualize drafting onto your team. This reflects another dimension of building your best team. It's a major component of the richness of what building successful relationships is all about.

Know You Are *FIRST*

Remember, it is important when someone calls you or shows up and says, "We have this project coming up, and I thought of you *first*." It's one thing to appreciate that in the moment, but this is a true celebration of your influence. This means that you now have begun the transformation of yourself and of your network. Now you have "Business Influence." Your network believes in you, trusts you, and is thinking of you *first*. You need to celebrate that!

When that began happening to me, it would bring up all kinds of self-doubt. I struggled to believe there wasn't another agenda other than the fact that they really appreciated me. I doubted that they knew I was doing the very best I could for people, that I care so much about people that I always do everything in my power to make sure that they will not fail, or the people they are bringing me won't fail.

It took me decades to realize this. I can still feel it coming up sometimes, like "This isn't real. It isn't okay for me to take this in. I'm just creating more emotional debt in the world that I'm going to have to service, and I feel it's a burden." Instead, flip it around. Know that you're *first*. Believe that. Celebrate it!

Power Move: *Journal and celebrate referrals and new business.*

Journal and celebrate those times when someone comes up and gives you their business, or brings you a referral you never asked for. Writing these special moments down helps you be thought of as *first*. You can journal in your phone, tablet, or a notebook. (Everybody has different places that they journal.) Make sure that you're serving yourself and feeling that shift in the fact that you're *first*.

Put Yourself *FIRST*. Then Put Your Team *FIRST*

When you're on a flight part of the attendant's instructions cover putting on oxygen masks, if necessary. You're always told to put the oxygen mask on yourself first, and then put it on your child or anyone else who may need assistance. That way you can think more clearly during an emergency and, therefore, be of more help to others.

The same concept applies with your team. By making sure you put yourself *first*, you will then be in good shape to help others. By doing this you're exercising good self-care.

It's more than okay in the celebration of things to go to your team and make that shift to where you're all collectively celebrating the things you've learned up to this moment. Celebrate that you've been co-creating this influence, building an amazing network and team, and emerging as a thought leader. Allow those feelings to come back to you. Your next step is to teach them what you've learned so they can become even stronger teammates for you, as well as becoming better people in the world.

Through Social Jack, we advise, "Teach your children, your family, friends, and colleagues" these skills. No matter what industry or career they end up in, this *first* mindset, skills, and practice will serve them well. Once you begin to teach this, you'll realize that you're not only a thought leader in what you do, but you're also a thought leader in creating business (and life) influence for others. Celebrate the fact that they are taking your lessons to that next level.

Power Move: *Constantly teach (influence).*

Sometimes, the realization of your teaching may take place in little movements. It may occur on social media or at a networking event. Once you start holding consciousness to this and effectively help others do that as well, not only do you become stronger, but your team grows stronger. Make sure you celebrate and listen for when your team takes the things that you've empowered them with and taught them. You hear them succeed with that. It's your time to help them celebrate their success.

This is a phenomenal dynamic. By employing your teaching abilities, you can change cultures, families, countries, even change the world

YOUR *NEXT* LEVEL
of Engagement

Build Your *NEXT* Level of Engagement

I hope you have enjoyed the wide variety of *firsts* that building digital business influence has brought your way. You'll find that as you practice the many strategies and tactics and develop your online networks, you will arrive at your *next* level of skill development.

One of these *next* level skills is that of engagement. Building your next level of engagement is key to growing successful networks. You'll likely feel fearful to, once again, reach out to others and build more opportunities for yourself and others. Many believe once they hit a certain level, that's all there is. But trust me, there is indeed more.

There is always a *next level* where you can explore deeper connections and, as a result, bigger opportunities for yourself and others in your networks. You've engaged with your team up to this point. Now it's time to venture out beyond your team to your team's connections and beyond. Reach out to people so far outside your network that you never imagined ever engaging with them. This is where social media can take your network and your results to the *next level*.

As I previously mentioned, I'm working on a new project focused on cryptocurrency, which I'm less knowledgeable about than many other areas. I began researching, and I found one of the top thought leaders in the world related to this space. In fact, he's one of the founding partners in much of the crypto movement. He just happens to be in Russia. I read some of his articles and engaged with him about the subject, out of the blue. It was magical that he engaged in return. He was deeply appreciative. We're now dialoguing on a more frequent basis.

This person showed up on LinkedIn as a third-degree connection. He was so far out of my network that I didn't have any common connections with him. I want you to explore the fact that if and when you're ready to reach out on this next level, you look beyond those you know. Move outside your comfort zones.

Power Move: *Look beyond your network for future team players.*

Look beyond your current network to connect to future players on your team, people who could be ideal networking partners. These people could be potentially on your next team. To engage with them, find one or two things in their profiles that you find highly commendable. Then, reach out via a tool like InMail offered by LinkedIn. Recognizing someone's gifts to the world in a kind and focused InMail could be just the vehicle to begin a long-term business relationship or even friendship.

Social media is ideal for finding, developing, and sustaining networking partnerships. You can choose to engage with a company, or one of their thought leaders and his/her content or directly with that thought leader/influencer. When you extend far beyond your current team and network, you'll be amazed at how you can draw in wonderful new connections and networks.

Upgrade to Your *Next* Team

Now that you are truly considering people farther out from your network—people with whom you have no mutual connections—you're in the process of upgrading to a next level. This can be a fun part, as you're to the point of considering: "What if I build another team?"

As you become increasingly successful, you'll grow new and different areas of influence that bring forth new, exciting projects. For instance, in tandem with the cryptocurrency project, I'm currently involved in a project called, "Ready for Next Cities." This is a group of leaders across the country who are joining efforts to help change every small business within certain cities and metropolitan areas. It's designed to be a large movement. It's just kicking off in its formative stages.

As I'm becoming part of this, I'm meeting new people and forming a separate team that doesn't necessarily have to do with Social Jack growing and getting funded. This is my nonprofit foundation to reach youth, our Digital Citizen program.

What you'll find interesting and fascinating is that some of your *next* teams might be completely separate. In fact, they very likely will be. They might be centered around initiatives that have to do with causes and organizations you're drawn to. They may be far outside what you're doing professionally, and possibly be about serving yourself or your passions. It could be charitable cause that you believe in. You can use everything that you've learned in this book to build that *next* team.

This is about assembling networks around things that move you, things you truly care about. You're upgrading yourself to having a *next* team. Make sure you don't just build a lot of teams and then not properly care for them. I'm adamant about making sure that you take care of your *first* team *first*. You can then move on to the *next* team(s).

Power Move: *Journal about what's next.*

Take a few minutes to write down and consider what you're working on, what you're drawn to next. What does your next team look like? Hold that vision for yourself of how you can apply what you've learned so far to be an influencer to that next team as you build it.

Have Fun Playing *NEXT* Players

As I described in the earlier sections on social teaming, the presence of play when you're with people (especially your teammates) is crucial. As you're building your next team and connecting to them, it shouldn't feel like work. To this end, remember to celebrate all along the way, as I shared in the last chapter. This is about you playing full out. You're all playing on the same mission, heading toward the same destination. There's mutuality in there, and it's fun.

As you begin to consider creating you next team, think about what backgrounds, values, etc. you would like to see in those new players. For instance, take a few moments right now to think about a cause that you sincerely care about. It could be world hunger, helping children, etc. Imagine that your next team will be the perfect players to help with that cause or mission. It could be your own foundation supporting another foundation or organization.

Then have fun playing your next players who are resonate with your new mission. Here you will find yourself as I shared in previous chapters, building with people get empowered by the same things you really care most about..

Power Move: *Keep playing with your team.*

Don't stress about needing to structure your entire *NEXT* team. Start by playing with them in the way that you know how now. Have fun doing it. Know that you're working on the same cause *together*.

Enjoy Your *NEXT* Level of Business Influence

In Chapter 8, I talked about celebrating your influence. Remember, however, that you should, simultaneously, always be in the process of re-evaluating your networks. You may well be at the point where you're developing multiple teams. Immerse yourself in the rich, rewarding feeling of success. Let your satisfaction simmer and seep into your soul.

Recognize that you are advancing your influence every day, with every outreach effort, connection, engagement, and interaction. Influence also continues with every meeting you have. Suddenly, your business influence is growing to the *NEXT* level. This can happen not just digitally but through your live meetings.

The difference between now and then is that you have learned you're truly a thought leader, a *business influencer.* Your personal brand has just transformed. Your thought leadership has transformed. Your world and your networks see you differently. Most importantly, you have transformed as a human being. Realize this isn't the end by any means. It's just the beginning.

There's a *next* level from wherever you are to wherever you're going, every step of the way. And you are never really finished. This world of social is all about practice toward mastery, and mastery never ends. By done, I don't mean you're done being an influencer. Rather, you've moved on to other arenas where you can influence.

Power Move: *Stay inspired.*

Never allow yourself to lose that drive. Don't give up hope or the realization that the system this book has taught you can always support you as you develop your *next* level of business influence.

Secret to the *NEXT* Level: Sustainability

The secret to what I call *next*-level sustainability translates to mastery of your business, your influence, your personal brand, your story, and your thought leadership. Here you also can achieve mastery of team building and of building community.

Whether that looks like reading this book over again or focusing on chapters you want to master, that's fine. Go with what works best for you. Once you have developed a habit of practicing the process I've shared in this book, at least two-to-five hours weekly, it's time to take your *next* steps.

These steps may include working with the accountability partner you've chosen. It may also include getting a coach to help you or electing to take supporting courses. Any of these steps help you move forward and upward.

True mastery happens when you are committed to practicing, daily, weekly, and monthly, the steps to achieving digital business influence mastery. Take the knowledge I've offered and commit to developing your skills to the next level. As you do this, don't forget to give yourself permission to enjoy the ride.

Also, remember to celebrate. And finally, realize you are not just seeking achieve the next level of business influence, but even more so, the next level of mastery.

Power Move: Become a master of success.

Achieve mastery of your living legacy by forming and building mutually beneficial relationships with others who hold similar values. These will be your partners, not just in the present, but throughout your life

ACKNOWLEDGMENTS

First, I thank my wife, Holly, for her unconditional love on this journey and for always believing in me during our hardest days. And my children, Sydney and Jackson, for allowing me the time to discover my purpose. To my parents Bob and Gloria, for being inspirational teachers; my sister Desiree and family, who inspired many of my roots, which have allowed me to fail and then succeed, and go on to share this knowledge with others. To my mother and father-in-law, for their love and influence.

Additionally, a special thanks to Melissa G. Wilson, my book-creation expert, for telling me a year ago we must do this, and then again, a few months ago, motivating me and helping me get my head and heart on paper. I also appreciate her whole team involved in this unique and powerful process.

To all my clients along the way (sorry, too many to mention all) who made this book possible: GE Global Companies, American Family Insurance, Southern California Institute, The Buona Companies, General Growth Properties, Centrust Bank, BNY Mellon, Indiana University, Chicago Mercantile Exchange, Morgan Stanley, Nationwide Insurance, Merrill-Lynch, Montro Homes, Real Estate Auctions, Sonixphere, Strazzeri Mancini, Century 21, Swiss Avenue Partners, InfoVera, UBS, Envestnet, Chicago Bears, University of Illinois, Wright Graduate University, The Founders Group, Wright Foundation, Union League Chicago, Chicagoland Chamber of Commerce, Naperville Chamber of Commerce, and Bansley & Kiener.

Additional thanks to the inspiration, support, and training from Zig Ziglar, Tony Robbins, Jim Rohn, Deepak Chopra, Drs. Bob and Judith Wright, Dr. Mike Zwell, Don Delves, Rich Lyons, Harry DeLisle, Bob Bouwer, Father Lazzar, James Grieco, Mark Schaefer, Joe Strazzeri, Steve Mancini, Shelley Lightfoot, Tom Meyer, Jim McMahon, Frank Montro, Pete Christman, Mosou, Jim Wolandi, Rachel O'Meara, Laura Stees, Miri Rodriguez, Elly Moody, Chris Rudolph, Ryan Pena, Erich and Jennifer Tengelsen, Darin Steen, Brian Kuzdas, Ken Monroe, Linas Jarasius, Larry Neems, Breanna Jacobs, Greg DeKalb, Andy Crestodina, Jon Ferrara, Jessika Phillips, Chris Strub, Chris Snider, Scott Snider, Mark Metry, Hank Conrad, Byron Mignanelli, David Carmen, Carl Kutsmode,Brian Jenkins, John Maxwell, Tony Paolella, Cait Hassett, Joe Karns, Sean Hutchinson, Barry Goodman, Daniel Popa, Dennis Synal, Mark Fentress, Jamie Dugan, Greg Allan, Dan Guzman, Michelle Lanter Smith, James Lumberg, Terry Trusgnich, The Nestor Brothers, Wayne Messmer, Billy Dexter, The Buonavolanto Family, Jiah Miesel, Marianne Floriano, Barry Kiesel, Spencer Maus, James Gough, Kevin Cieslak, Paul Engelbrecht, Todd Bredar, Aaron Breford, Bob Gustas, Russ Bereolos, John Warta, Angie and Paul Lowe, Barry Waxler, Richard Hollis, James Gustin, Kim Kislowski, Mary Patchin, Elene Cafasso, KC See, Mark Schaefer, Purdue University, DePaul University, Chicago Computer Learning Center, Freddy's Steak House, and the Children's Home and Aid Society.

When you create a network, you don't just touch one soul at a time, but 8,000 souls at once..

BEFORE YOU GO

It was such as honor to spend these hours with you as you read this book. I'd like to take just a few more minutes to make two requests.

First, if you enjoyed this book, would you be so kind as to take a moment, go to Amazon, look up the title, and leave a brief review? Books succeed by the kind, generous time readers take to leave honest reviews. This is how other readers learn about books that are beneficial for them to buy. To this end, I thank you in advance for this very kind gesture of appreciation. It means the world to me.

Second, please reach out to someone that you see has a need for the things you learned in the pages of this book. It's my mission to influence the world, one student at a time.

Finally, please stay in touch. To this end, visit my website: www.deandelisle.com and sign up to receive updates on both this book and other things I am creating to help you build your digital business influence.

Made in the USA
Columbia, SC
12 September 2019